Protection

for voluntary organisations

Paul Ticher

In association with
Bates Wells & Braithwaite
solicitors

DIRECTORY OF SOCIAL CHANGE

Published by
Directory of Social Change
24 Stephenson Way
London NW1 2DP
Tel. 08450 77 77 07; Fax 020 7391 4804
email publications@dsc.org.uk
www.dsc.org.uk
from whom further copies and a full books catalogue are available.

Directory of Social Change Northern Office
Federation House, Hope Street, Liverpool L1 9BW
Policy & Research 0151 708 0136

Directory of Social Change is a Registered Charity no. 800517

First published 2000
Second edition 2002
Third edition 2009

ISBN 978 1 903991 92 3

British Library Cataloguing in Publication Data
A catalogue record for this book is available from the British Library

Cover design by Kate Bass
Text designed by Kate Bass
Typeset by Keystroke, Wolverhampton
Printed and bound by Page Bros, Norwich

Contents

Contents

Contents

Contents

Acknowledgements

The author would like to thank everyone who has contributed to the book, especially those participants on training courses and briefing sessions whose acute questions and real-life examples have done so much to stimulate his thinking about Data Protection.

Special mention must also go to Lawrence Simanowitz, a partner at Bates Wells & Braithwaite Solicitors, for reading the book in draft and providing a welcome legal perspective, and to Sandy Adirondack for providing up-to-date information for Appendix A (and many other pieces of legal background through her website, www.sandy-a.co.uk). Any remaining errors and misunderstandings are, of course, the responsibility of the author alone.

Third edition

This third edition includes additional and revised material based on experience with the Act during the five years since the second edition came out. It takes account of new and updated guidance from the Information Commissioner, key cases in which the courts have delivered interpretations of various aspects of the Act, policy developments and other legislation which impinges to a greater or lesser extent on Data Protection.

Important note

This edition aims to take account of legislation and case law up to the end of September 2008. However, please note that this book does not set out to be a full statement of the law, and is not a substitute for professional legal advice on specific issues. Bates Wells & Braithwaite Solicitors can be contacted via their website www.bwbllp.com. Details of the current legislation in force may be found at www.statutelaw.gov.uk.

Now that the 1998 Data Protection Act has been in force for some years, a few high-profile court cases have addressed some important aspects of the Act. However, the Act's interpretation is often more of an art than a science. Much of it has not been tested in the courts. The most official interpretation is based on guidance from the Information Commissioner. While authoritative, this is not legally binding. It is quite possible that the Commissioner's guidance might change, or be overturned by legal decisions.

Foreword

Data protection issues are more relevant today than ever before. Increasingly, charities are seeing their supporters engage with them in multiple ways including donating, volunteering and campaigning. These complex relationships that supporters now have with our cause demand that we take data protection even more seriously. It has never been more challenging or important to speak to supporters as individuals

Managing data well is important to everyone in a charity but from my perspective as a fundraiser it is certainly the case for several reasons.

Firstly, it is our responsibility to ensure that our fundraising complies with all relevant legislation. This handbook is indispensible in setting out clearly and concisely our legal responsibility and what is considered to be best practice.

But there is another crucial reason why fundraisers should be interested in data protection: managing data effectively is the key to good relationship fundraising and can help you to increase your income.

It is a well-established fact that the success of a fundraising appeal will be determined as much by to whom it is sent as by the proposition it contains. In a highly competitive market, maintaining the support and good will of our supporters is critical. Honouring requests, communicating personally and offering choice plays a large part in making people feel valued and respected.

This handbook offers practical guidance on a wide range of data protection issues to any charity concerned with protecting the personal data of their clients and service users, as well as their supporters. It can help you and your organisation ensure that you are not only fulfilling your legal responsibilities but also using data to build more meaningful and productive relationships with your supporters.

Ruth Ruderham
Head of Fundraising
Christian Aid

About the author

Paul Ticher is a consultant and trainer working with national and local voluntary organisations. He specialises in information technology and good practice in information management, with a particular interest in Data Protection. Much of his work experience has been in the advice and information field, including five years as IT Adviser at the Community Information Project (now absorbed into London Advice Services Alliance), where he undertook a considerable amount of work on the application of the 1984 Data Protection Act to voluntary organisations when it was first introduced. He has also worked in campaigning organisations and as Chief Officer of a small national charity.

Since the first edition of this book appeared in 2000, Paul has been a leading trainer on Data Protection throughout Britain, and he has advised many voluntary organisations on the subject.

Readers are invited to contact the author with comments, or to seek further help on issues which are not adequately covered here.

e-mail: paul@paulticher.com

Definitions and abbreviations

Terms used in this book are defined briefly below and explained in more detail on the pages indicated.

The Act – the Data Protection Act 1998.

Computer – used as a shorthand term in several places in this book. The Act refers to 'equipment operating automatically in response to instructions given for that purpose'.

Data – information held on computer or, in many cases, on paper, including photographs, video material, etc., *see pages 20–21*. In this book 'data' is treated as singular, like information, since this is becoming the accepted practice. Quotations directly from the Information Commissioner treat 'data' as a plural, and this has not been changed.

Data capture – the process of obtaining information from the **Data Subject,** either on paper forms or verbally, often used in the context of the **Data Controller**'s first contact with that person.

Data Controller – the organisation (or, occasionally, individual) responsible for how and why Personal Data is used, *see Chapter 2*.

Data Processor – an organisation (or, occasionally, individual) to whom data processing has been outsourced, *see page 15*.

Data Protection Commissioner – the original name of the official responsible for enforcing Data Protection law under the 1998 Act, known as the Data Protection Registrar before 1 March 2000, now the Information Commissioner.

Data Protection Principles – the eight Principles which set out a Data Controller's main responsibilities under the Act when processing Personal Data, *see Chapter 5*.

Data Protection Registrar – *see Data Protection Commissioner, above*.

Data Subject – an individual about whom Personal Data is held, *see Chapter 4*.

Definitions and abbreviations

Direct marketing – 'the communication (by whatever means) of any advertising or marketing material which is directed to particular individuals', *see Chapter 12.*

Information Commissioner – the official responsible for enforcing Data Protection and associated law. At the time of writing, the Commissioner was Richard Thomas. In this book the Commissioner is therefore referred to as 'he'.

Notification – the name under the 1998 Act for the equivalent to Registration under the 1984 Act. Most, but not all, Data Controllers have to 'notify' the Information Commissioner about the broad outline of their data processing activities.

Personal Data – information about a living individual who is identifiable from the data held on them by a Data Controller, *see Chapter 3.*

Privacy and Electronic Commerce Regulations 2003 (often abbreviated to PECR) – the regulation under which electronic marketing (i.e. by e-mail, telephone, fax and text message) is regulated, *see page 79.*

Processing – any use of Personal Data, including obtaining, storing, using, disclosing or destroying it, *see page 35.*

Record – used in this book to mean a set of information about one individual.

Relevant filing system – manual (paper) files subject to the Data Protection Act, *see page 24.*

Sensitive Personal Data – special categories of data which have to be treated with special care, *see page 47.*

Subject Access – the right of an individual to have a copy of the information a Data Controller holds about them, *see Chapter 13.* This should not be confused with the right granted by the Freedom of Information Act 2000, of access to non-personal information held by a public authority, *see Chapter 16.*

Introduction

Data Protection

Data Protection can come over as terribly dry and procedural, but it goes to the heart of individual concerns – with a potentially serious impact on people's lives. If your GP transfers your records to computer and the old paper files end up in a skip for anyone to see, that's a Data Protection issue. If your bank confuses you with someone else and your credit rating plummets, that's also a Data Protection issue.

'Data Protection' is in some ways a misnomer which has impeded good understanding of the legislation. For it is not, at heart, about protecting data: it is about protecting people. Specifically, it is about protecting people from the consequences of their data being misused, mishandled or mismanaged.

These consequences can be severe – to the extent of physical harm or even death. Fortunately, such extreme effects are rare. The challenge for those managing voluntary organisations is to achieve the right balance: taking appropriate steps to prevent rare but potentially serious events, without imposing a regime which is so restrictive that it hampers the effective operation of the organisation.

The Data Protection Act 1998 recognises this tension and allows a balanced approach, but there is a clear onus on managers to think carefully about the measures that are appropriate in their particular circumstances. Data Protection is not just a matter of following a limited set of prescriptive rules.

The Act offers genuine rights to Data Subjects as well as providing a framework for responsible behaviour by those using Personal Data. While no legislation is ever 'perfect', the Act is generally workable and reasonable.

The Data Protection Act is not, however, generally well understood. There are three main reasons for this.

- It is genuinely complex, covering a number of separate issues under the broad area of the way Personal Data is managed, used and protected.

- The Act itself does not clearly state its underlying objectives. (This is a feature of most legislation, but in this case it seems particularly unfortunate, since the objectives are not immediately or intuitively obvious.)

- Much of the implementation is based on complying with the eight Principles set out in the Act – where a number of courses of action might achieve the same end result. Different organisations may decide to take different approaches, each in itself acceptable, but confusing when compared with each other.

This last element – having to make decisions about how to comply with the Principles – also means that for organisations it is not just a matter of adopting, or even adapting, a standard set of policies and procedures. The best course of action will depend on what the organisation does and the way it does it, and therefore needs to be closely tailored to the specific needs and practices of that organisation.

While the main concern of the Act is to prevent harm, close behind this comes the concept of 'fairness' – above all being open and honest with the Data Subject on how you are using information about them, and in some cases giving them a choice over what you do with the data. This is mainly intended to address people's legitimate worries about privacy and intrusion in an age when information about them can be manipulated and shared widely through the power of computers.

Fairness also means using people's data in predictable ways, looking after the data and taking care that it doesn't get into unwelcome hands. And who could argue with that? It's no more than we would expect from anyone who holds data about us.

For voluntary organisations, openness and fairness is also key to building a relationship of trust with a wide range of people who are vital to the effective functioning of the organisation, including clients, volunteers, donors and paid staff – an activity which is not just desirable, but essential. Good Data Protection practice can also demonstrate to funders and regulators that the organisation's responsibilities are taken seriously.

Because of this, voluntary organisations have no reason to fear the Data Protection Act. In many ways it gives legal backing to good practices that have long been practised in the sector. It also provides a framework for thinking through and addressing the risks and areas of concern, so that Data Protection Officers can be sure that their organisations have policies and procedures that genuinely protect the interests of Data Subjects.

This book makes the assumption that voluntary organisations will be keen to follow best practice wherever possible. Indeed, it is often more onerous to make the effort to find technical loopholes. Such grudging compliance is an option, of course, for those wishing to circumvent the spirit of the Act. As with any law, there are grey areas and special cases that can be exploited to avoid giving people the maximum benefit from the law. Ignoring the legislation is increasingly not an option, however, as the Information Commissioner starts to tighten up on enforcement and Data Subjects come to expect, and insist on, greater transparency and higher standards of compliance.

Good Data Protection practice is unlikely to be very far from what most voluntary organisations are doing already. However, it is always worth considering whether risks, or opportunities for better practice, have been overlooked, and there are also specific compliance issues – including a few bureaucratic requirements – to be aware of. There are even a very few circumstances in which Data Protection considerations may appear to conflict with what the organisation would really prefer to do. These are discussed at appropriate points in the book.

Structure of the book

This book does not strictly follow the structure of the Act. It starts with an overview of the steps that most organisations are likely to have to take to bring themselves into compliance. It then looks at the Act in more detail.

The first few chapters deal with the definitions of the key players in Data Protection: the Data Controller, the Data Subject and the Data Processor; and the essential concept of 'Personal Data': the type of information that the Act applies to.

Chapter 5 then outlines the eight **Data Protection Principles** on which Data Protection is based, followed by a series of chapters which explore in more detail what each of these Principles could mean in practice for voluntary organisations.

The next few chapters explore themes that cut across a number of Data Protection Principles – communicating with Data Subjects, confidentiality and privacy, the Internet, and collaborative working with other organisations.

Finally there are chapters on a few technical aspects of the Act – notification and enforcement – and more detailed suggestions for organisations wishing to take action to review or improve their Data Protection practices.

Background

The United Kingdom got its first Data Protection law – fittingly, as it seemed at the time – in 1984, the year of George Orwell's Big Brother. The law was introduced in order to allow the government to ratify a Data Protection Convention that had been drawn up by the Council of Europe. The limitations of the 1984 Act quickly became apparent. For organisations that were using data about people it imposed bureaucratic burdens, while offering very little benefit to individuals who might be concerned about how their data was being used.

Very early in the life of the 1984 Act, criticisms began to emerge. At its heart it did very little to promote good practice in the use and management of Personal Data. Although it was based on fairly sound Data Protection principles, it allowed a Data User[1] to do more or less anything they wanted, provided that it was legal and that they had registered with the Data Protection Registrar in very broad terms what they intended to do.

The information a Data User had to provide when registering was so general and unspecific that it gave very little information to anyone seriously interested in finding out anything about a Data Processing operation. At the same time, filling in the forms was confusing and frustrating, and – particularly for small voluntary organisations – the registration fee was a significant disincentive. Hardly surprisingly, only an estimated 40% of those legally required to register actually did so.

A Data Subject wanting to check up on the data held about them could be faced with paying one organisation several, or in some cases even dozens, of £10 fees in order to cover all the possibilities. It was said that to see all the information held on one person by the Metropolitan Police could have cost £350.

On top of all this, the enforcement powers of the Data Protection Registrar were limited. Despite the heroic efforts at persuasion by successive Registrars and their judicious use of the legal powers available, Data Protection under the 1984 Act never had much real day-to-day impact.

The limitations of the 1984 Act were widely acknowledged within a short time, and pressure grew for the most obvious problems, at least, to be ameliorated. However, the Home Office took the view that it did not want to legislate again in this area too quickly. Quite soon, the European Union began debating harmonisation of its Data Protection laws, and this was then given as a valid reason for making no change in the UK, only to have to make another set of changes once the European position was finalised.

Unfortunately, while the debate in Europe dragged on well into the 1990s, the Home Office steadfastly stood by its decision to wait. Even the most obvious changes could not be made without recourse to Parliament because the very fine detail of the 1984 Act was enshrined in the primary legislation itself. Successive Data Protection Registrars did the best they could – for example to simplify the registration process – but had very limited room for manoeuvre.

Eventually, on 24 October 1995 the European Union agreed Directive 95/46/EC on the harmonisation of Data Protection laws. This gave member states three years to enact domestic legislation to put the Directive into effect. The UK government was still unenthusiastic about Europe, and dragged its feet – even for a while considering minor amendments to the 1984 Act rather than the wholesale revision that was merited.

---

1 Under the 1984 Act a Data User was any organisation or person who 'holds or controls' Personal Data. The 1998 Act equivalent is a Data Controller.

For some, this turned out to be a blessing in disguise, as it gave a clean start to the new government which took office in May 1997. Commendably quickly, in August 1997 a White Paper appeared, committing the government to implementing the spirit as well as the letter of the European Directive. This was followed, after a short period of consultation, by a Bill which had its first reading in January 1998.

Instead of incorporating all the detail into the Bill, as had been done in 1984, the 1998 legislation laid down a broad structure, leaving much of the detail to be completed through secondary legislation. This has the important advantage that if changes have to be made in future, they can be brought in much more easily, without the need for a new law. We should no longer have to live with unworkable provisions merely because the effort of changing them is judged not to be worth it.

However, an unfortunate consequence was that Royal Assent for the new law on 16 July 1998 was not the end of the story. The law could not take effect until some 30 pieces of secondary legislation had been prepared, consulted on and brought before Parliament. Despite the deadline set in the European Directive, the UK – in common with most other EU member states – started to fall behind schedule. In fact it was 1 March 2000 before the Act finally came into effect. Another step closer to the final stage was taken on 24 October 2001, when the main transitional period ended and the new regime came almost fully into force, but it was not until 24 October 2007 that the final 'transitional provisions' expired. These related to paper records that had been held before October 1998 and had very little practical impact.

There have been minor changes to the Act since it came into force. The Freedom of Information Act 2000, in particular, introduced potential conflict over whether information relating to individuals should be made public. The result is that public authorities have to disclose more information to a Data Subject than other Data Controllers. The Freedom of Information Act also took the opportunity to tidy up a number of other small matters. Further amendments were made in the Criminal Justice and Immigration Act 2008.

There have also been a few court cases that affect interpretation of the Act. These, and changes to the legislation itself up to September 2008, are fully taken into account in this edition.

Has all the effort been worth it? There is no doubt that the current legislation does overcome many of the most obvious flaws in the old (1984) Act.

- Data Subjects are given real, if limited, controls over how their information is used.
- There is provision for much greater transparency: Data Subjects should know much more now about who is doing what with information about them.
- The impenetrable and unhelpful format for registration has been replaced with a slightly simpler system of notification.

- Above all, the Act now incorporates much good practice. In the past, complying with the Act and following good practice, while by no means mutually exclusive, were almost two separate exercises.

The new Act requires all those who use Personal Data – not just those who hold it on computer and not just those who have to notify – to be careful, fair and responsible in the way they use it.

Whatever its flaws and problems, the 1998 Act is a much better starting point for all concerned – both those who use data about people, and the people whose data is being used.

Chapter 1

Approaching Data Protection

Data Protection compliance is not usually about following a set of discrete rules. Your activities as a whole have to produce the right result, and you have to take a broad view over all your areas of work to ensure that this is the case.

This chapter:

- Sets out a suggested course of action for any organisation wishing to review its compliance with the Data Protection Act

As discussed in the Introduction, at the heart of Data Protection are two main concerns, each of which leads to two main requirements.

- Preventing harm to individuals, which means:
  - keeping information only in the right hands;
  - holding data whose quality is fit for purpose.

- Demonstrating respect and allaying individuals' concerns, which means:
  - ensuring that you are transparent about your activities;
  - giving people choices, where this is relevant and possible.

The Data Protection Act itself does not state its objectives so baldly, but is based on eight Data Protection Principles. The bulk of this book is taken up with looking at what compliance with these Principles might mean in practice.

Instinctively, most voluntary organisations would comply with perhaps 90% of the Data Protection Act, even in the absence of legislation. This is because voluntary organisations believe in, and often actually exist to promote, individual rights. Strict client confidentiality is already a central concern for most voluntary organisations, and the vast majority have no interest in exploiting or upsetting their staff, donors, volunteers or other contacts.

The first message is therefore not to panic or worry unduly. In many voluntary organisations existing practice will not have to be changed much to bring it into line with the legal requirements in the Act. You are likely to be achieving compliance in many areas already by common sense and a basic respect for the Data Subject.

This book also suggests that Data Protection compliance should not necessarily be based on a single, comprehensive Data Protection policy. Instead, existing policies and procedures – on confidentiality, security, case recording or marketing, for example – should be reviewed to ensure that they are Data Protection compliant. This offers the best prospect of keeping Data Protection close to everyday operations and meaningful to the staff who have to operate within it, rather than having a set of ambitions sitting in a dusty file which is never opened.

Having decided to tackle Data Protection, you will probably need to work in three broad areas:

- clarifying responsibilities and specific legal obligations;
- carrying out an audit and identifying areas where action is needed;
- ensuring that all your paid staff and volunteers who have contact with Personal Data understand their responsibilities.

In all this, your main concerns should be:

- **Security** – being confident that all your staff and volunteers, trustees or committee members will maintain confidentiality and ensure that data is not used inappropriately.
- **Data quality** – so that data is fit for purpose: adequate, relevant and accurate.
- **Transparency** – making sure that your Data Subjects are not kept in the dark about what you are doing, especially about non-obvious uses of their data or conditions under which you would disclose their data to other people.
- **Data Subject rights** – in particular the right to opt out of direct marketing, which includes fundraising and other unsolicited contacts.
- **Reliable, consistent systems and procedures** – so that when a Data Subject gives consent, expresses a preference or tells you that their data has changed, this is recorded accurately right across the organisation.

Responsibilities

In terms of responsibilities and legal compliance, you are likely to have to address all or some of the following points.

- Identify the Data Controller, or Controllers, in respect of all the Personal Data you handle (see Chapters 2 and 3). Normally your organisation will be the Data

Controller. In addition, if you have a trading subsidiary, that will most likely be a Data Controller in its own right. Where you have a complex organisational structure, or work closely with other organisations, things may not be so straightforward.

- Ensure that your board or management committee is aware of its responsibilities for Data Protection compliance and makes any necessary decisions.

- Nominate a senior post to have an overview of Data Protection within your organisation.

- Clarify the Data Protection responsibilities of department heads, team leaders and other relevant staff.

- Review your employment contracts and volunteer agreements to ensure that Data Protection responsibilities are adequately covered.

- Review your contractual arrangements with any Data Processor to which you outsource work (see Chapter 2).

- Ensure that your notification is accurate and up to date (see Chapter 21). This can only really be done after you have carried out your audit.

Audit

The style of audit recommended by the Information Commissioner can be lengthy, detailed and time consuming. You may eventually decide that this is appropriate for you. Initially, however, you need to get an idea of what is most urgent, by identifying your main likely problem areas. Suggestions for how to do this can be found in Chapter 23.

This process is likely to throw up questions that need to be resolved. You may need advice from your umbrella body or from an external professional, or you may just need to make certain decisions – for example whether to seek consent from certain Data Subjects for some of the uses you want to make of their data.

Some of these decisions and other Data Protection compliance measures should be recorded in an appropriate policy or operational procedure – for example decisions on whether you will charge for Subject Access and who will handle Subject Access requests to your organisation. Your audit should aim to identify which policies or procedures – either existing ones or ones you decide to create – need some Data Protection content.

Your policies (see Chapter 23) should not necessarily be lengthy documents, but should clarify the standards you wish to meet, in terms that make sense both to your Data Subjects and to your staff. You may also need to spell out specific procedures designed to achieve your standards. For example, you may want all parts of your organisation to use consistent phrasing when they offer people a marketing opt-out.

Training

Training for your staff and volunteers can then be based around the appropriate policies and procedures for their area of work. Short training sessions, repeated for new staff and with refreshers once or twice a year, are better than long, detailed sessions that are never followed up. Often these training sessions are best carried out at the team level, where people can discuss case studies that are particularly relevant to their work.

The following chapters explain the Act in more detail.

Chapter 2

Who is the Data Controller?

Legal responsibility for compliance with the Act lies with the Data Controller. Normally this will be an organisation, not individual staff or volunteers. If you outsource any activities that involve the use of (or access to) Personal Data, you are dealing with a Data Processor.

This chapter looks at:

■ How to identify the Data Controller, particularly in more complex situations where this may not be straightforward

■ The relationship between a Data Processor and your organisation

The concept of the Data Controller is a fundamental element in the 1998 Act. If you are a Data Controller, the Act applies to you in its entirety. If you are not a Data Controller, your responsibilities are much more limited. You need to be clear, therefore, in every situation who is the Data Controller.

The definition appears, at first sight, quite straightforward. The Data Controller is whoever decides why and how Personal Data is to be processed.

Data Controller

A Data Controller is defined as 'a person who (either alone or jointly or in common with other persons) determines the purposes for which and the manner in which any Personal Data are, or are to be, processed'.

The first point to note is that the definition uses the word 'person', not 'individual'. In other words, a legal 'person' – such as a limited company – can be a Data Controller in its own right. An unincorporated organisation is not a legal person,[2] which would appear to mean that such an organisation cannot be the Data Controller.

The view favoured by many lawyers is that each individual on the management committee or board of trustees would technically be a Data Controller, acting 'jointly' with the others.

However, the practice under the 1984 Act was to allow unincorporated associations to register in the name of the organisation, rather than under its trustees acting jointly, and the Information Commissioner has indicated that this approach is to continue.

The Information Commissioner's legal guidance[3] says that: 'a data controller must be a "person", i.e. a legal person. This term comprises not only individuals but also organisations such as companies and other corporate and unincorporated bodies of persons.' The Information Commissioner's staff have expanded on this[4] and stated that, having taken QC's advice, an unincorporated organisation can, legally, be a Data Controller, 'however any formal legal action . . . would be taken against the legal persons who make up the governing or controlling mind of that organisation, and not against the unincorporated organisation in its own name'.

In other words, for most day-to-day purposes you can probably behave as though an unincorporated organisation is in fact the Data Controller. However, it is as well that your committee or trustees are made aware of the precise situation, and the potential – however remote – for legal action against them as individuals. If in any doubt about what this means, you should take qualified legal advice.

Our parent body has told us that its notification will cover us for Data Protection. Is this OK?

Probably not. You cannot *choose* to be a Data Controller on someone else's behalf. The question is, 'Where are the decisions made?'. If you are given strict instructions by your parent body, and have no leeway, then it could well be the Data Controller. However, if the local organisation is independent enough to make its own decisions and set up its own systems it is more likely to be a Data Controller in its own right.

---

2 Don't forget that whether your organisation is incorporated or not has nothing to do with whether it is a charity. It could be both incorporated and a charity, or one and not the other, or neither. See Appendix A for a note on this issue.
3 A lengthy document, available on the Information Commissioner's website.
4 Correspondence with the author, dated 15 June 1999.

Joint activities and consortia

There are situations where two organisations, acting jointly or in common, are Data Controllers of the same Personal Data.

As a general guide, the likely situation is that if two or more organisations are using the same data for the same purpose(s) they will be 'joint' Data Controllers. Either could be liable to pay compensation for any breaches of Data Protection, even if the mistake was actually made by the other Data Controller. If they are pooling data to use for different purposes – for example where they each have separate data about the Data Subject that only the originating organisation can see and use – they will be acting 'in common', liable only for their own actions. For example, you may be organising a conference in collaboration with another organisation, deciding together on the 'purposes' for which the Personal Data is collected and the 'manner' in which it is processed. Both organisations will share the responsibility as joint Data Controllers.

It is increasingly common for several organisations to get together in a formal consortium and agree to share client data, so that a person known to one organisation in the consortium does not have to provide their details all over again when they approach another. If they share just the basic contact details, but then add their own specific case records, it is likely that the organisations would each be Data Controllers, acting in common – but they could end up carrying some of the responsibility if another member of the consortium breached the Act. The implications of collaborative work are explored further in Chapter 20.

When might an individual be a Data Controller?

An individual employee is most unlikely to be the Data Controller of Personal Data that is used by an organisation in the course of its activities. The Data Controller will – in the vast majority of cases – be the organisation itself. The staff member will merely be an agent of the Data Controller. This is explicit in the Act.[5]

An exception to this is where the individual has a right to retain personal information for their own purposes. This was the subject of a High Court case in 2007,[6] in which it was decided that a journalist had the right, in certain circumstances, to develop his own list of contacts even when he acquired them in the course of his employment. This would make him a Data Controller for that contact list.

The case may be less clear-cut when it comes to volunteers or to self-employed people who carry out a particular service for the organisation. Members of the Information Commissioner's staff have indicated that they believe that volunteers should be treated

---

5 In s.1 the definition of 'Data Processor' specifically excludes employees of the Data Controller – see Data Processors, page 15.
6 Pennwell Publishing (UK) Ltd v Ornstein and others EWHC 1570 (QB), [2007] IRLR 700.

as agents of the Data Controller, in exactly the same way as employees. This appears reasonable, even though it is not made explicit in the legislation. Employees, volunteers, agency staff and contract workers are all likely to be agents of the Data Controller.

Self-employed people, however, may well be Data Controllers in their own right. Organisations should ensure that any transfer of data to freelance workers or other external contractors complies with the Data Protection Principles (see Chapter 5).

Does my private wedding invitation list make me a Data Controller?

No. The Act does not apply to genuine domestic use of Personal Data. Someone using a computer to maintain a wedding invitation list is, in effect, totally exempt. This exemption does not apply, however, if you handle Personal Data, even at home, on behalf of an organisation, even a small, informal, voluntary one with no money and no staff. Even holding a card index recording the birthdays of children who attend your local playgroup could make you a Data Controller. (But the Data Controller would be the playgroup if it had asked you to do this.)

Where there is a serious possibility of confusion, it is likely to be worth establishing the situation very clearly on paper – possibly through your contract if you are paying people for services. Again, qualified legal advice is strongly recommended.

Even though individuals are clearly not Data Controllers when they are acting as agents for an organisation, many organisations will wish to identify a specific staff member or member of the governing body as Data Protection Officer. This person will have a clear responsibility to inform themselves about Data Protection issues, to ensure that the organisation complies with its obligations, and to train or brief other staff in what they are and are not allowed to do and what to do if they are in any doubt. This is covered in more detail in Chapter 24.

I work with partner organisations abroad. Are they Data Controllers?

The UK Act only applies to organisations that have a base, or process their data, in the UK. If your partners are independent, they will be subject to their own local Data Protection law, if any. If the relationship is not totally independent, it would be worth taking advice. See also Chapter 15.

Data Processors

Instead of, or even as well as, being a Data Controller, an organisation may be a Data Processor. This is defined in the Act.

Data Processor

Data Processor means 'any person (other than an employee of the Data Controller) who processes the data on behalf of the Data Controller'.

The Act goes on to lay down conditions applying to a Data Processor. The key points are as follows.

- The relationship must be clear and the Data Processor must be following directions from the Data Controller. If it has any discretion at all (other than exercising professional judgement in carrying out the wishes of the Data Controller), the chances are that the organisation might not be a Data Processor but a Data Controller in its own right.
- There must be a written contract between the Data Controller and the Data Processor.
- The Data Controller must satisfy itself that the Data Processor's security is appropriate, and must enforce adequate security through the contract.

Note that an individual – such as a freelance worker or other contractor – can be a Data Processor, which is especially likely if they are providing a service to your organisation in return for money.

The important point is that the Data Controller remains responsible for what happens to the data, and remains liable for any mistakes. If you outsource your payroll, for example, your employees would still quite rightly complain to you if they didn't get paid. You, not the Data Processor, would have to compensate them if they incurred bank charges as a result. Your remedy would be to have provision in your contract with the Data Processor for it to reimburse you. Otherwise you would just have to accept your loss as the penalty for choosing a less than perfect supplier of payroll services.

Typical examples of Data Processors include not just payroll companies, but also marketing and fulfilment houses, telemarketing bureaux, computer maintenance companies (if they have direct access to the organisation's Personal Data), and even companies undertaking secure destruction of confidential records.

Some commercial organisations offering services that mean they are likely to be Data Processors will have incorporated the necessary provisions into their standard contracts. However, it is the Data Controller's responsibility to ensure that compliant contractual arrangements are in place.

2) Brian is a keen member of his local church. Without consulting anyone, he plans to build up a small database on his home computer of people who are likely to help with the annual Christmas Fair. Just in time, he realises that this will make him a Data Controller. He decides it would be better if the church were the Data Controller, so hands over control before starting the project.

3) A mediation service uses self-employed sessional mediators. The case notes are recorded by the mediators and kept by them. The service knows which clients are on which mediators' case-list, but holds no further details. The service has strict rules on confidentiality but makes no other rules about what information should be recorded or how it should be kept. This raises the possibility of each individual mediator being the Data Controller for the information they hold (depending on how they hold it). After consultation, the organisation decides that it would be better to issue clear instructions to the mediators about what to hold and how, including rules on security and confidentiality, to make it clear that the organisation is the Data Controller.

4) Veronica is in charge of fundraising at a large charity. In addition to mailing its previous donors, it has a contract with a specialist telephone fundraising agency which calls people to ask for money. Because there is a written contract, and because this makes it clear that it is the charity which makes all the decisions (about who to call and how often, for example), the fundraising agency is a Data Processor, with the charity remaining the Data Controller at all times. However, Veronica has also developed a small 'Friends of the Centenary Project' group of volunteers. She gives them the names and details of the 500 top donors and says, in effect, 'Raise as much money from these people as you can, in whatever way you think best.' Unless she makes this relationship more formal, she realises that in this case the group of volunteers would almost certainly be a Data Controller in its own right.

Chapter 3

What is Personal Data?

Whatever information you hold about people, most of it will be subject to the terms of the Data Protection Act. But in some instances – largely arising when the information is held on paper – the Act does not apply. The easiest option may be to assume that, for most purposes, all personal information is covered. That way, you can't go wrong. You may, however, feel you need to know more about the scope of the Act in certain situations.

This chapter explains:

■ How to work out which types of information are covered by the Data Protection Act and which are not

The 1998 Data Protection Act is concerned with 'Personal Data'. To be covered by the Act, information must be 'personal' and it must also be 'data', as defined by the Act. This leads to some anomalies, as we shall see, because no matter how personal the information is, if it is not 'data', the Act provides no protection. The diagram and the box defining 'data' overleaf may help to clarify this.

The 'personal' part of the definition is relatively straightforward, referring to data about:

■ identifiable • living • individuals.

It therefore does not apply to information about companies or organisations, but could apply to named contacts within those organisations. It does not apply to data which is completely anonymous, but it does apply if you can identify the people from

	Data	Not data
Personal	The Act applies	The Act does not apply
Not personal	The Act does not apply	The Act does not apply

the data combined with other information you hold. It does not apply to information about people who have died, and it does not apply to fictitious people.

'Data' is a trickier concept. It is defined in the Act under four headings and a fifth was added in the Freedom of Information Act 2000. The full definition is given in the box, but for most voluntary organisations data essentially amounts to:

- information held on computer;

- information in 'relevant' manual files;

- information intended to become part of one of the above systems.

'Computer' is used above as shorthand to include any computer-based equipment.

Data[7]

Data means information which:

(a) is being processed by means of equipment operating automatically in response to instructions given for that purpose;
(b) is recorded with the intention that it should be processed by means of such equipment;
(c) is recorded as part of a relevant filing system or with the intention that it should form part of a relevant filing system;
(d) does not fall within paragraph (a), (b) or (c) but forms part of an accessible record as defined by section 68;
(e) is recorded information held by a public authority and does not fall within any of paragraphs (a) to (d).

[Note: Category (d) relates only to records held by medical professionals and by schools, housing and social services run by local authorities. 'Public authorities' in category (e) are those covered by the Freedom of Information Act (see Chapter 16).]

---

7 See paragraph 1 of the Act for all definitions quoted in this and the following chapter.

It is particularly important to note that 'data' does not just mean text. Photographs and video recordings, in particular, must now be treated much more carefully if they relate to identifiable, living people, as must biometric data in many cases. See Appendix D for a short discussion of some of the issues that might arise with photographs and videos.

You should also think about less obvious places where personal information might be held, such as the phone numbers stored in your mobile phone or personal digital assistant, or the computer log that records individuals' access to a building protected by a swipe-card entry system.

Just because these might be Personal Data, it doesn't necessarily follow that you are doing anything wrong at the moment. But, to be sure, you do need to review your practice.

> **I have a database of organisations. Surely the names of my contact people don't count?**
>
> Actually, they do. You probably know their name, their employer, their job title or position, their direct phone line, their e-mail address, and possibly more. This makes the information 'personal'. It is held on computer, so it is 'data'. However, the consequences of this being Personal Data are usually minimal, provided you use the information in obvious business-related ways. You do have to be more careful with very small voluntary organisations: the contact details they give you may be someone's home address and phone number.

> **If I overhear a conversation between two clients, does the Data Protection Act apply to what I do with that information?**
>
> Not unless you write it down. It doesn't matter how 'personal' it is; it can only be 'data' if it is *recorded* (either on computer or in a relevant filing system).

The Durant case and EU Opinion 4/2007

In December 2003 the Court of Appeal ruled in the case of Durant v Financial Services Authority.[8] Among other things, the court looked at what makes data 'personal' and the definition of a 'relevant filing system'.

Although the Court's ruling has to be recognised as the current state of the law in the UK, it may not be the end of the story. Many commentators, both in the UK and at the European level, were astonished at the narrowness of the interpretation favoured

---

8 Michael John Durant v Financial Services Authority [2003] EWCA Civ 1746, Court of Appeal (Civil Division).

What is a 'relevant filing system'?

The Directive applies to manual systems only 'if the data processed are contained or are intended to be contained in a filing system structured according to specific criteria relating to individuals, so as to permit easy access to the Personal Data in question'.

It then goes on to define a 'Personal Data filing system' as 'any structured set of Personal Data which are accessible according to specific criteria, whether centralised, decentralised or dispersed on a functional or geographical basis'.

The definition that the UK government put in the Act was significantly different.

Relevant filing system

Relevant filing system means 'any set of information [not on a computer] relating to individuals to the extent that . . . the set is structured, either by reference to individuals or by reference to criteria relating to individuals, in such a way that specific information relating to a particular individual is readily accessible'.

The interpretation of this definition was another major feature of the Durant case. The Information Commissioner's guidance on Personal Data indicates the intention to produce a parallel guidance note on 'relevant filing system', but it had not appeared at the time of writing.

The Appeal Court in the Durant case stressed that each element of the definition must be taken on its own, and that ease of access to specific information is paramount.

The Information Commissioner's original guidance on this (which will eventually be superseded by the guidance mentioned above) suggests the 'temp test'. In other words, if a temporary worker, or new member of staff, with no special knowledge of where any specific information was located could easily find any specific piece of information then the system is probably a relevant filing system.

If, for example, personnel files are organised so that each member of staff has a file, and within that their holiday records can always be found in the same place, then a temp could easily answer the question of how many days' holiday a particular member of staff had taken so far this year and the files would qualify as a relevant filing system.

Be wary, however, of assuming that manually held data is outside the Act. Even if the file is disorganised, the more easily you can look up information about specific individuals, the more likely it is to be Personal Data. For instance, if you put the booking forms for your training courses into files course by course, but have a separate index of who has attended each course, these forms could well be Personal Data.

Note that the information must be in a 'set'. A single phone number on a sticky note wouldn't be covered, but an alphabetical list of personal phone numbers might be.

Is it Personal Data?

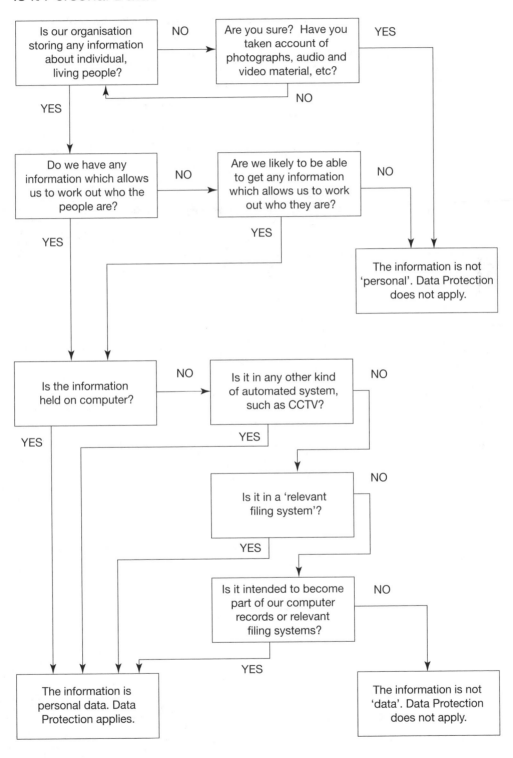

Information intended to go onto computer or into the files

There are potentially important consequences from the fact that material intended to form part of a computer or manual system is data. What this means is that the 'data capture' documents on which you collect information come within the scope of the Act, even if you discard them as soon as the data is in your system. Application forms, booking forms (which may include credit card details) and interview notes are just some examples of what could be covered by this element of the Act.

All the responsibilities of Data Controllers – to act fairly, to ensure appropriate security and not to keep data longer than necessary, for example (as discussed in later chapters) – apply with equal force to these 'data capture' documents.

Consequences of the definition of Personal Data

Some personal information is never going to be covered by the Data Protection Act – information that is overheard and not recorded, for example. Other information appears to be excluded from the Act by virtue of not falling strictly within the definition of 'personal' or 'relevant filing system', even though the consequences of it being mishandled could be serious.

As a result, many organisations have concluded that for some purposes it is good practice to extend protection to more than just Personal Data. A clear example is an organisation's approach to confidentiality, which is addressed as a specific topic in Chapter 17.

In other cases it would be prudent to recognise that the situation is still fluid, and to assume that the definition of Personal Data may in future become broader than it currently stands in the UK. It is not usually worth expending energy to find arguments for excluding information from the provisions of the Act if good practice suggests that it should, in fact, be treated responsibly anyway.

Summary

Although the definition of Personal Data is not as clear-cut as one might like, most information that voluntary organisations hold about people will be Personal Data, and therefore covered by the Act.

In the vast majority of cases there will be no dispute. Examples include:

- client or case records;
- records of staff and volunteers;
- membership records;
- newsletter mailing lists;
- fundraising or supporter databases;
- training administration records (whether for external or internal courses);

- most conference administration and bookings systems;
- contact databases (unless they contain information exclusively about organisations, with no named individuals);
- computer-based sales records, where the purchaser's details are kept;
- lists of consultants, trainers or other resource people.

The two key questions are: is it 'personal', and is it 'data'? If the answer to both is 'yes', then the set of information is covered by the Act.

Even where information about individuals is, or may be, outside the definition, it is often good practice to treat it as though it were, in effect, covered.

Examples

1) Maria runs a befriending service which uses a couple of dozen volunteers. When anyone applies to be a volunteer they fill in a form, which is then filed. There is a separate file for each volunteer, and they are in alphabetical order. Holiday records and training records are also kept in these files. Should Maria treat the files as Personal Data?

   She quickly realises that in this manual system she can easily find specific information about particular people, and therefore that it should be treated as Personal Data.

2) Martin has a complaints file where complaints are received from individuals. Much of the content is highly sensitive, so he might expect Data Protection rules to apply automatically.

   However, the file is merely in date order, according to when each complaint was received, with no index. Martin concludes that it probably does not fall within the definition of data. He cannot go to the file with the intention of finding information about a specific, known individual.

   On the other hand, were he to reorganise it so that the complaints are filed in alphabetical order of the person who complained, then the likelihood is that it would be covered.

   There is even a third possibility: if all the complaints about each member of staff were filed together, then the set of information might be Personal Data about the staff members rather than about the complainants.

3) Rajan is surprised to see a Data Protection statement in the reception area of a big multinational company that is hosting a conference for his organisation. It uses closed-circuit television (CCTV)[12] to monitor each area of the office for security purposes and the company's security manager has decided that the contents of the tapes may well be Personal Data. To be safe, the company publicises this prominently.

4) A telephone helpline takes a lot of details about its callers, but allows them to remain anonymous. Susan, the operations manager, transfers the information to computer so that she can analyse the pattern of calls. Is the information on computer Personal Data? What about the paper records of calls?

Susan realises that if all the information on the computer is anonymous and there is no way of identifying the people via other information (on paper, for example), then the computer database is not Personal Data. The paper records might be Personal Data if they include the names of people who rang up and they are filed so that individual people's records can be easily found, in which case the computer record would also be Personal Data.

5) William is a personnel manager in a large charity. He gets a lot of people writing in asking about employment. They are each sent a personalised, wordprocessed letter, and their enquiry is put in a file called 'employment enquiries'. When a vacancy comes up, someone looks through the file and sends details of the job to anyone who looks suitable. William wonders whether the 'employment enquiries' file might be Personal Data? And what about the wordprocessed reply letters?

Eventually William decides that the 'employment enquiries' file is not Personal Data. Technically, he thinks that the wordprocessed letters could be Personal Data, even if the personalised letter is not saved. (In practice, however, he realises that the consequences of the letters being Personal Data are likely to be minimal.)

---

12 CCTV was the subject of one of the first Codes of Practice issued by the Information Commissioner under the 1998 Act. It has subsequently been revised and a supplementary checklist issued for small users. These are available on the Commissioner's website.

Chapter 4

The Data Subject

A Data Subject is anyone whose Personal Data is processed. Normally it will be clear who your Data Subjects are, but some records can be complex, holding information about more than one person. Normally the Data Subject will act on their own behalf, but it is possible for others to act for them.

This chapter:

- Explores who might be a Data Subject
- Clarifies how other people can act on behalf of your Data Subjects

The Data Subject

Most of your records will clearly be about specific individuals: clients, donors, supporters, employees, volunteers or contact people in other organisations, for example. Where the record is about a single individual, the situation is usually clear, but any particular record may contain information about more than one individual, and in many cases both or all of the individuals will be Data Subjects.

For example, you may deal with a family rather than an individual. If your records contain information about more than one member of the family each is likely to be a Data Subject in their own right, with all the rights this involves (as described in later chapters). They also have the right to be treated as individuals; there may be confidentiality issues (see Chapter 17) about sharing information concerning one family member with another.

While you may be able to identify most of your 'primary' Data Subjects without difficulty, it is worth paying attention to the inadvertent creation of 'secondary' Data Subjects. For example, in a personnel system, your staff will clearly be Data Subjects. However, you may ask them for details of next of kin, or emergency contacts.

If these details are put onto computer, the additional people are also likely to be Data Subjects.[13]

If your personnel records are in manual files the emergency contacts may not be Data Subjects because you can't 'readily' find out anything about them; you can only go by the staff member's name on the file. However, if you routinely collect information about the partners and children of staff members and keep this in a standard section of the manual personnel files, there may be a case for deciding that these people could be readily located.

Data Subjects can also be people who have provided information about someone else. Someone who provides a reference, for example, may be a Data Subject if their name goes onto your computer. Even if it doesn't, they generally have specific rights if the person about whom they have provided information wants to see their file (see Chapter 13).

> **I only have information about people overseas. Are they Data Subjects?**
>
> Yes. There is no geographical restriction.

In the remainder of this book, 'Data Subject' should be taken to mean 'Data Subject or someone legitimately acting on their behalf'. The situations in which someone might be able to act on behalf of someone else are now discussed.

Authorisation to act on behalf of a Data Subject

Whenever an individual exercises their Data Protection rights or is asked by you to make a decision – giving consent to a particular use of their data or to a disclosure, for example – in most cases the Data Subject will be able to deal directly with you. However, they don't have to: someone else may be entitled to act on their behalf, they can ask someone else to act on their behalf, or you may decide that it is appropriate for someone else to act on their behalf.

The person acting on behalf of the Data Subject should normally be properly authorised, and, if acting on behalf of a Data Subject who does not have capacity (discussed further below) must act in the Data Subject's interests. If you are not confident that these two conditions apply, then you should not automatically accept the request or decision.

In many cases you would be looking for formal, legal authorisation.

- An adult may authorise someone else to act on their behalf for a specific purpose.
- Someone with a power of attorney can act on someone else's behalf.
- A parent can act on behalf of a child who is too young to act on their own behalf.

---

13 This does not automatically mean that you have to tell these people that you have their data, but you do have to treat the information responsibly (see Chapter 19).

The most clear-cut case is probably where an adult asks someone to act on their behalf – engaging a solicitor, for example. It would not be unreasonable for you to ask to see a signed authorisation from the Data Subject if there is any doubt. In practice, however, this is rarely felt necessary, and the solicitor's assurance that they act for the individual is normally taken at face value.

An adult who is not capable of making their own decisions – either temporarily or permanently – may have appointed someone under a lasting power of attorney to act for them in such a situation. The Mental Capacity Act 2005, which came into force on 1 October 2007, widened the range of issues on which a power of attorney can be exercised. In cases where the risk is low, you may decide to accept an assurance that a power of attorney exists. If in doubt, however, or if the matter concerns money or raises some other potential risk, you should consider asking for evidence.

In the case of children, in Scotland the Data Protection Act provides that a child is normally deemed capable of exercising their own rights from the age of 12. In England, Wales and Northern Ireland, because of differences in the legal system, the requirement is just that they must have sufficient understanding to act on their own behalf. The presumption must be that they are similarly capable, and that they are therefore likely to be able to act for themselves around the age of 12.

When children are not old enough (or otherwise not competent) to act on their own behalf, a person with parental responsibility as set out in the Children Act 1989 can act on their behalf, but must still be acting in the child's interests. In very rare cases you may feel that a parent's actions are not in the child's interests – or that information you hold about a child should not be disclosed to the parents for some reason – but it would normally be wise to take professional legal advice in such a situation.

Acting in the absence of authorisation

There are many situations where formal authorisation is either non-existent or the evidence is not available to you. In such cases you may have to make a judgement as to whether the person seeking to act on behalf of the Data Subject is appropriate. Many commercial companies take the approach that no risks must be taken and therefore refuse to have dealings with anyone who is not the Data Subject. This can lead to considerable irritation, for example when someone makes a phone call in connection with a bill, only to find that the company will not deal with them because the bill is in the name of someone else in their household.[14]

This approach is likely to over-cautious and unhelpful in most voluntary sector settings. However, care must be taken neither to divulge information inappropriately nor to enable someone to interfere inappropriately with another person's affairs.

---

14 The Information Commissioner makes this point regularly. A statement was issued in September 2008, for instance, setting out some of the myths which result in organisations failing to respond appropriately to requests for information, and giving examples where people had been seriously inconvenienced by a too-strict interpretation.

You cannot even assume that it is always appropriate to share information with a Data Subject's spouse, or for them to act on behalf of their husband or wife. People are allowed to have secrets from each other – and you wouldn't even want to spoil an innocuous surprise.

To avoid individual staff having to make a judgement on the spot, it is worth considering the most likely situations that people in your organisation are likely to face, and coming up with guidance to cover these, leaving any unusual situations to be dealt with on a case-by-case basis – possibly by reference to a manager or other appropriate person.

The best approach is to try to pre-empt problems as far as possible by establishing with the Data Subject at the outset who else might act on their behalf. For example, when you are taking on a new client or signing up a new supporter you could ask whether they are happy for you to deal with anyone else in their absence – if you phone them to check something, for example – or who else they are happy for you to disclose information to if you are unable to give it to the Data Subject directly. This is especially relevant if your client's condition is likely to deteriorate over time, or if they are in a particularly stressful or upsetting situation.

Even if you do this, there will still be situations where no prior arrangement has been made. You are just as entitled as a commercial company to refuse to deal with anyone other than the Data Subject, but this is often unhelpful. Several points may help in producing your guidance.

- Try to ensure that you know who you are talking to. It may be reasonable to make some checks – such as asking them to give you a piece of information which you can verify, and which would only be known by someone close to the Data Subject.

- Try to avoid disclosing more information than necessary about the Data Subject, unless you are sure that the person you are talking to is appropriate.

- Consider sending a confirmation of the discussion directly to the Data Subject by some other means. That way, if it turns out that you have made a mistake, at least the Data Subject will find out straight away.

It may also be helpful to consider the principles set out in the Mental Capacity Act 2005[15] when your Data Subjects are adults who are not necessarily able to make their own decisions. Paraphrased, these principles are as follows.

- You must assume that people have the capacity to make their own decisions until it is proved otherwise.

- You must take all practicable steps to help people make decisions for themselves.

- People can make an unwise decision if they want to – that doesn't mean they are unable to make their own decisions.

---

15 This does not apply in Scotland, which has separate legislation in this area.

- Anyone who does intervene must act or decide in people's best interests.
- Anyone who does intervene must minimise any restriction on people's rights and freedom of action.

Summary

- A Data Subject is anyone whose Personal Data is processed.
- When identifying Data Subjects, you must take into account *all* the people you have information about, not just your primary Data Subjects.
- Anyone acting on behalf of a Data Subject should be authorised, and if acting on behalf of a Data Subject who does not have capacity, must act in the Data Subject's interests.
- Children can normally act on their own behalf from around the age of 12.
- There are various formal means of authorising people to act on behalf of both adults and children.
- You need to be careful in dealing with someone who has not been formally authorised to act on behalf of the Data Subject, but it is usually unhelpful to refuse to deal with them at all.

Examples

1) Alice's organisation has a category for 'family membership'. The names of everyone in the family are listed on the membership application form. Staff are told that if for any reason they phone a household which has family membership, they can assume that everyone in the family is aware of the membership. This means that they can talk to anyone who is old enough to understand the conversation, if their name appears as a member. It doesn't have to be the person who signed the form or paid the subscription.

2) A medical self-help group is aware that its members' condition may deteriorate over time. When people first become members – and at intervals after that – they are asked to give (or confirm) the names of anyone close to them that they would be happy for the organisation to talk to about their condition. This is carefully recorded, but the group always tries to deal directly with the members, only using the alternative contact if the member is unable to communicate.

Chapter 5

The Data Protection Principles

Everything you do with Personal Data has to comply with the eight Data Protection Principles contained in the Data Protection Act. Each Principle is explored in more detail in later chapters.

This chapter gives:

- An overview of the eight Data Protection Principles in the Act

At the heart of the Data Protection Act is the list of eight Data Protection Principles. These Principles apply to *every* Data Controller, even one that only processes a small amount of manual data. They also apply to *all* processing. Everything you do with Personal Data has to comply with all the Principles.

It is important to understand that the Principles are not fixed rules. In any situation there may be more than one course of action that would comply. This makes life more difficult in some ways; each organisation has to consider carefully how it will comply with the Principles – and it can lead to confusion if two organisations make different decisions about the same situation. On the other hand, having the flexibility to decide how to comply does mean that Data Protection requirements need not be a bureaucratic burden.

Processing

Before going on to look at the Principles, it is necessary first to examine the Act's definition of 'processing', since this sets the scope of the Act's application.

Processing has been defined in the Act effectively to include anything at all that may bring you into contact with Personal Data: from collecting it, through holding, using, changing, copying, disclosing or passing it on, all the way through to destroying or erasing it.

It is hard to imagine any activity related to the holding or use of Personal Data which does not count as processing.

> **Processing**
>
> Processing . . . means obtaining, recording or holding the information or data or carrying out any operation or set of operations on the information or data, including:
>
> (a) organisation, adaptation or alteration of the information or data,
> (b) retrieval, consultation or use of the information or data,
> (c) disclosure of the information or data by transmission, dissemination or otherwise making available, or
> (d) alignment, combination, blocking, erasure or destruction of the information or data.

The Principles

Principle 1 concerns 'fair' processing and sets out in some detail the actions that Data Controllers must take, as well as conditions they must meet, in order to avoid being unfair. Unfortunately, it cannot be fully understood without reference to Schedule 2 and Schedule 3 of the Act (Schedule 1 covers the Principles themselves). For this reason the Principles as they stand do not lend themselves easily to being used for briefing staff on how to work within the Act. Some ideas on how to present the Act to staff and volunteers are given in Chapter 24.

Principle 2 requires that data must only be obtained for a 'specified' purpose or purposes. The purpose can be 'specified' in one of two ways: by 'notifying' the Information Commissioner (see Chapter 21) or by telling the Data Subject directly.

Principle 2 also contains the important provision that all your processing must be compatible with the purpose(s) for which you obtained the data. This means that you cannot, for example, disclose information to someone else unless you are sure that the disclosure is compatible. Even within your organisation, if your service is confidential you must restrict access on a need-to-know basis. A management committee member leafing through the client files, just because they felt like it, would probably breach the second Principle.

The Data Protection Principles[16]

1   Personal Data shall be processed fairly and lawfully and, in particular, shall not be processed unless:
    (a) at least one of the conditions[17] in Schedule 2 is met, and
    (b) in the case of sensitive Personal Data, at least one of the conditions in Schedule 3 is also met.
2   Personal Data shall be obtained only for one or more specified and lawful purposes, and shall not be further processed in any manner incompatible with that purpose or those purposes.
3   Personal Data shall be adequate, relevant and not excessive in relation to the purpose or purposes for which they are processed.
4   Personal Data shall be accurate and, where necessary, kept up to date.
5   Personal Data processed for any purpose or purposes shall not be kept for longer than is necessary for that purpose or those purposes.
6   Personal Data shall be processed in accordance with the rights of data subjects under this Act.
7   Appropriate technical and organisational measures shall be taken against unauthorised or unlawful processing of Personal Data and against accidental loss or destruction of, or damage to, Personal Data.
8   Personal Data shall not be transferred to a country or territory outside the European Economic Area unless that country or territory ensures an adequate level of protection for the rights and freedoms of Data Subjects in relation to the processing of Personal Data.

The standard 'purposes' set out by the Information Commissioner for the purposes of notification are broad, and a single purpose can encompass a wide range of activities. Examples of purposes[18] include the following.

- Staff administration: appointments or removals, pay, discipline, superannuation, work management or other personnel matters in relation to the staff of the Data Controller.

- Consultancy and advisory services: giving advice or rendering professional services. The provision of services of an advisory, consultancy or intermediary nature. You will be asked to indicate the nature of the services which you provide.

- Fundraising in support of your objectives.

- Processing for not-for-profit organisations: establishing or maintaining membership of, or support for, a body or association which is not established or

---

16 Schedule 1, Part I of the Act.
17 See the following chapter for more about the conditions in Schedules 2 and 3.
18 These are quoted from the Information Commissioner's *Notification Handbook: a complete guide to notification.*

conducted for profit, or providing or administering activities for individuals who are either members of the body or association or have regular contact with it.

- Realising the objectives of a charitable organisation or voluntary body: the provision of goods or services in order to realise the objectives of the charity or voluntary body.

Principles 3, 4 and 5 essentially insist that data should be of good quality. While there may be specific cases in which it is hard to draw a clear line, most Data Controllers would in any case want to follow these Principles.

Note that it is up to the Data Controller in the first instance to decide what is 'necessary', although there may be legal considerations, especially about how long it is necessary to keep Personal Data.

In Principles 3 and 5 the decision on whether the data meets the criteria must be taken in relation to the purpose(s) for which it is being processed.

Principle 6 covers Data Subject rights. These include the right of access to their data, including manual files, and the right to prevent processing in certain cases – in particular where harm is being caused to the individual, or where direct marketing is concerned. (For more details on this, see Chapter 12.)

Principle 7 imposes a duty to have appropriate security, again applying to manual as well as computerised records. You may have to restrict access to files by staff or volunteers, unless they have a good reason, as well as by people outside the organisation.

'Organisational' security measures should include drawing up policies and procedures and training staff to follow them. 'Technical' measures include physical access control, such as locks on doors and filing cabinets, as well as things like computer passwords and back-up procedures.

When a Data Controller 'notifies', they have to provide certain information about their security measures.

The question of security is addressed further in Chapter 14.

Principle 8 has from time to time caused considerable disagreement between the EU and the USA, and it appeared at one point as though data transfer between the EU and the USA (as well as most other countries) would be seriously hampered by this principle. The commercial ramifications would have been inestimable, and a political solution was required. See Chapter 15 for more details.

Summary

- All 'processing' of Personal Data must be 'fair'.
- You must collect and use Personal Data for specified purposes only.

- The data must be adequate, relevant and not excessive.
- The data must be accurate and up to date.
- The data must not be held longer than necessary.
- Data Subjects' rights must be respected.
- You must have appropriate security.
- Special rules apply to transfers of Personal Data abroad.

Examples

1) Nirmal's advice agency receives most of its funding from the local council, under a contract. One year the council announces that it is changing the conditions of its contract. To ensure that the funds are spent only on eligible clients, it wants to inspect random case records as part of its monitoring procedure.

   Nirmal and his colleagues are understandably upset at the thought that the council officers may be seeing their confidential records, and worry about the effect this might have on clients. They wonder if they can refuse on Data Protection grounds.

   One issue here is whether disclosing the records to the council officers (which is certainly 'processing') is compatible with the purpose(s) for which the data was originally collected. Would the agency be breaking the second Data Protection Principle?

   Nirmal looks into it and decides provisionally that the agency has a case for refusing access. If the monitoring were for quality control, it would be possible to argue that this was an integral part of providing the service, and it therefore would be compatible with the original purpose. But auditing the agency's use of funds is a separate activity. The agency therefore asks the council to reconsider, and to look for a way of monitoring that does not involve breaches of either client confidentiality or Data Protection.

2) Melissa runs an organisation that promotes good childcare. Over time it has built up a database of many of the local childminders, which it uses to send out relevant information and invitations to training events. The organisation gets a lot of phone calls from people asking if they can recommend a childminder in the area, but the organisation is reluctant to do this. Instead, it considers publishing its database as a list which people could use to make their own selection.

   However, Melissa points out that in her view this is a completely different purpose from the original one of providing direct services to the childminders. If the organisation wants to do this, she feels that it needs to go back to the people on the database and, in effect, collect the data anew for this new purpose.

3) A community transport organisation starts to get comments from its drivers that they need to have more information about the service users in order to provide a good service. If they knew that someone needed help getting from their door to the vehicle, for example, the drivers could get out straight away and offer the help. They argue that it is relevant to providing the service, and therefore compatible with the third Data Protection Principle. The management committee agrees and decides to collect this additional information from service users who are happy to give it.

The committee also decides that it needs to be careful not to collect too much data. It doesn't actually need to know the person's specific disability, just the kind of support that they might need. So the organisation redesigns its record forms to ask very direct questions: 'Do you want the driver to come to your door to assist?' 'Can you get into the vehicle without the hoist?' 'Will you normally have a dog with you?'.

4) Some of the users of the Afro-Caribbean Elders Day Centre are reluctant to reveal their ages. Michael, a former volunteer worker, was embarrassed about asking this, so he used to guess when filling in the database. After a talk by the council welfare rights officer, the centre realises that some of its users could be claiming age-related benefits. Joyce, the centre manager, agrees that this use of data is within the original purpose, so she agrees to search the database for users over a specific age.

The first problem is that the database has been set up to record the age of the person when they first started using the centre. These ages have not been updated, so the centre is in danger of breaking the fourth Data Protection Principle: the data is not kept up to date. For now, the staff realise that they can work out the current ages by seeing how long the person has been a user, but for the future they decide to change the database so that it records date of birth and calculates the current age, rather than recording a specific age.

Then they find that some of the ages Michael has guessed turn out to be under-estimates. When Joyce pulls off a list of people to talk to about the benefits they may be entitled to, some of those who should be invited to the talk get missed off. These people find out that their friends are claiming a benefit that they are not, and some of them complain. This could be another breach of the fourth Data Protection Principle: the data is not accurate. Joyce decides to make it very clear to volunteers from now on that they must not guess. If they don't know the answer, they must leave the field blank or enter a specific 'don't know' value (and the database must be set up so that this is possible). In this way, if the centre is doing a similar exercise in future, the staff can make sure that those whose ages they don't know also get invited to the talk.

Chapter 6

Fair processing

Everything you do with Personal Data has to comply with the eight Data Protection Principles contained in the Data Protection Act. Each Principle is explored in more detail in this and later chapters.

This chapter looks at:

- The need to ensure that the Data Subject is informed, and the occasions when it is fair not to inform them
- The 'conditions' for fair processing and the circumstances in which you can process data without consent

If the Data Protection Act can be summed up in one sentence, it is probably in the first Principle: 'Personal Data shall be processed fairly'. All processing has to be fair, and the Data Controller has a general responsibility for fairness above and beyond the specific requirements discussed here.

In addition, it has to be processed lawfully. For voluntary organisations this means, in effect, that any processing that breaks a law other than the Data Protection Act is automatically unfair (for example if record-keeping provisions in the Care Standards Act 2000 Regulations or National Minimum Standards are not adhered to). For statutory bodies it is more complicated, as they must have a specific power to carry out every action they undertake. Without it, their actions are *ultra vires* and therefore unlawful. This has, on numerous occasions, raised problems concerning data sharing, and using data for multiple purposes. See Chapter 20.

The first Data Protection Principle

Personal Data shall be processed fairly and lawfully and, in particular, shall not be processed unless–

(a) at least one of the conditions in Schedule 2 is met, and

(b) in the case of sensitive Personal Data, at least one of the conditions in Schedule 3 is also met.

The Act goes into some detail about what the first Principle means. It is particularly concerned with how you collect or otherwise obtain Personal Data and with 'transparency' – how you ensure the Data Subject knows enough about what you are doing.

The first Principle should be read alongside the second. This says that you must have a 'specified' and lawful purpose or purposes for obtaining data, and one of the things you have to be particularly transparent about is your purpose(s).

The second Data Protection Principle

Personal Data shall be obtained only for one or more specified and lawful purposes, and shall not be further processed in any manner incompatible with that purpose or those purposes.

Transparency

Transparency is the main requirement for fair processing. If the Data Subject would be surprised to find out that you have data about them, or surprised by what you are doing with it, then you have almost certainly failed to be sufficiently transparent.

This transparency should extend to:

- the fact that you have information about the Data Subject;
- all the purposes that you use it for, especially any that are not obvious;
- who you might disclose it to;
- how the Data Subject can exercise any rights they have to obtain information or to place restrictions on your use of the data.

You may provide this information in any appropriate way, but it has to be available before the Data Subject commits to giving you their information or, if you get it from someone else, as soon as reasonably practicable. Except in the cases discussed below, it is likely to be unfair to use data about people in any way without their knowledge, and without being open about who you are and how you can easily be contacted.

The Act makes it clear, in particular, that data has not been collected fairly if:

- anyone has been deceived or misled in the process;
- the Data Subject does not know (or cannot readily find out) who is processing the data and what they intend to do with it.

In addition, the Data Subject has to have 'any further information which is necessary [in the circumstances] to enable processing . . . to be fair'. The 1995 European Directive gives examples of what this 'further' information might be. These include:

- the recipients or categories of recipients;
- whether data provision is voluntary or mandatory;
- the existence of the right of access.

This does not necessarily mean that you have to go to great lengths to tell people about why you are collecting their data: it may be obvious. For example, when you take on a new member of staff and ask them for their bank details so that you can pay them, a Data Protection statement is likely to be superfluous.

However, you do have to take care where any intended use of the data is not immediately obvious. Even if you have specified the non-obvious purpose by notification to the Information Commissioner, you still have to ensure that the Data Subject knows what is going on before the processing can be fair. In particular you need to make the Data Subject aware if you intend to make any non-obvious disclosure to a third party – for example if some of the services you offer are actually delivered by someone else and you need to pass on member or client details for this to happen, or if you have any intention of passing details to another organisation which may use them for contacting the individual directly.

Many voluntary organisations' existing policies in areas such as client information and confidentiality will already go beyond the letter of the Data Protection requirements. However, in some cases practices may need to be changed, particularly where contact with clients is made over the telephone or by e-mail, or through a third party acting on behalf of the organisation. The practical implications of this are discussed in Chapter 19.

Processing without the Data Subject's knowledge

Where you obtain Personal Data from someone other than the Data Subject themselves, the Data Subject is still entitled to know who you are and what you are doing, unless this would require 'disproportionate effort'. This is almost the only ground on which the information may be withheld. See Chapter 19 for a discussion on this.

If you are relying on the 'disproportionate effort' exemption, you have to keep a record of your reasons for believing the argument applies.[19] You must also provide the information to anyone who asks for it. (Remember that this exemption does *not* apply to data you get directly from the Data Subject, only to data you obtain from someone else.)

---

19 This rule was added to the Act by Regulation (Statutory Instrument 2000 No. 185, paragraph 5), although in practice it seems that few Data Controllers comply (or are even aware of the requirement).

My staff sometimes have to make home visits where there is a risk of violence. Can I put a violent warning marker on the client's file? And do I have to tell the client?

Yes, you can indicate the risk, because Data Protection does not override your duty of care towards your staff. However, you also have to be as fair as possible to the client. Unless you think it would increase the risk, you should tell them what you are doing, and explain why. You should be careful about how you phrase the warning and you should also have a procedure for reviewing the situation at reasonable intervals. You should also make sure that the only people who see the warning are those who need to.

Conditions for fair processing

The first Principle refers to the 'conditions' for fair processing that are set out in Schedule 2 of the Act, and are quoted in full in the box below. Data processing is not considered fair unless it meets at least one of these conditions.

1 The Data Subject has given consent.

2 Processing is necessary to carry out a contract to which the Data Subject is a party.

3 Processing is necessary to meet a legal obligation of the Data Controller.

4 Processing is necessary to protect the vital interests of the Data Subject.

5 Processing is necessary for various judicial and government functions.

6 Processing is in the legitimate interests of the Data Controller or someone they disclose information to – unless it causes undue harm to the Data Subject's rights, freedoms or legitimate interests.

Conditions relevant for purposes of the first principle: processing of any personal data (Schedule 2 of the Act)

1 The Data Subject has given his consent to the processing.
2 The processing is necessary–
   (a) for the performance of a contract to which the Data Subject is a party, or
   (b) for the taking of steps at the request of the Data Subject with a view to entering into a contract.
3 The processing is necessary for compliance with any legal obligation to which the Data Controller is subject, other than an obligation imposed by contract.
4 The processing is necessary in order to protect the vital interests of the Data Subject.

5 The processing is necessary–
  (a) for the administration of justice,
    (aa) for the exercise of any functions of either House of Parliament,[20]
  (b) for the exercise of any functions conferred on any person by or under any enactment,
  (c) for the exercise of any functions of the Crown, a Minister of the Crown or a government department, or
  (d) for the exercise of any other functions of a public nature exercised in the public interest by any person.
6 (1) The processing is necessary for the purposes of legitimate interests pursued by the Data Controller or by the third party or parties to whom the data are disclosed, except where the processing is unwarranted in any particular case by reason of prejudice to the rights and freedoms or legitimate interests of the Data Subject.
  (2) The Secretary of State may by order specify particular circumstances in which this condition is, or is not, to be taken to be satisfied.

The first condition, consent, is discussed in Chapter 8. For the other conditions, 2 to 6, the processing must be 'necessary' for the stated purpose. It is up to the Data Controller to judge in the first place what is necessary.

The Information Commissioner has indicated that 'vital interests' (Condition 4) should be interpreted very narrowly, as 'life or death' emergencies. It should not be used routinely. Many voluntary organisations may want to make the case that situations such as actual or potential homelessness, harassment, abuse and threats of serious violence are also 'vital interests'. As things stand, however, this is not the Information Commissioner's interpretation (see also the following chapter).

While all processing has to meet at least one of the six conditions, not all instances of processing the same set of data need meet the same condition.

- Data collected with consent might subsequently be used without consent to protect the vital interests of the Data Subject, provided that this is compatible with the original purpose for which it was collected.

- Data collected in connection with a contract might be used in the interests of the Data Controller (for example if staff details were provided to an employer's liability insurer), again provided that this was compatible with the purpose(s) specified at the time when the data was obtained.

- Some people on a contact database may have given consent (by asking to be kept in touch), while others may be there on the grounds of the Data Controller's

---

20 Added by the Freedom of Information Act 2000.

legitimate interests (for example because they are local councillors), without having consented.

It is very hard to envisage any reasonable activity in most voluntary organisations which would fail to meet at least one of the conditions. The requirement to meet the conditions is therefore unlikely to impose any major burden. The important point is that the Data Controller must be able to say, if the question is raised, which condition (or conditions) they are relying on.

We do a lot of work under contract to the council. Are we carrying out 'functions of a public nature' and therefore covered by Condition 5(d)?

Probably not. Following a court case in 2002 involving the Leonard Cheshire Foundation, it appears that even where a voluntary organisation is providing statutory services under contract to a local authority, this does not amount to carrying out a 'public function' in relation to the Human Rights Act 1998. It would be logical to assume that the same would apply to the similar terms in the Data Protection Act.

However, this may change. There are, for example, at the time of writing, moves to extend the application of the Human Rights Act to non-statutory bodies delivering statutory services[21] and possibly to extend Freedom of Information obligations to a wider range of organisations. If this trend continues, voluntary and commercial organisations may increasingly find themselves regarded as carrying out public functions.

Summary

All processing of Personal Data must meet at least one of six conditions. It must take place:

- with the consent of the Data Subject;
- in connection with a contract involving the Data Subject;
- to meet a legal obligation;
- to protect the Data Subject's 'vital interests';
- to fulfil a wide range of government functions; or
- in your 'legitimate interests', provided that the Data Subject is not unduly harmed.

---

21 There is provision in s.145 of the Health and Social Care Act 2008 for non-statutory bodies running care homes to be made subject to the Human Rights Act, but it was reported in July 2008 that the Ministry of Justice intends to consult before implementing this.

In the case of R (Weaver) v London and Quadrant Housing Trust [2008] EWHC 1377 (Admin) it was found that a social landlord was a public authority, and therefore subject to the Human Rights Act, largely because it was housing people on behalf of the local authority.

Examples

1) The staff of a sheltered housing scheme find that some of the residents are being bombarded with marketing material after filling in a lifestyle questionnaire. They decide to help the residents complain on the grounds that they were misled about the purpose of the survey, and that the processing of their data is therefore unfair.

2) A council for voluntary service (CVS) maintains a database of local organisations, with details of contact people. The information officer, Jane, is unsure whether she can keep these contact names without consent. She is quickly reassured that this use of the data is likely to fall under condition 6: it is in the legitimate interests of the Data Controller and the Data Subjects are not being harmed (they gave their names voluntarily as contact people, after all). However, if the CVS was in the business of publishing a directory of local organisations, it would need to consider whether those contact people who had given their home address, for example, could be included without consent. The details of the organisations themselves, of course, are not covered by Data Protection.

3) Barry is the secretary of a small charitable trust which gives money to individuals in the locality. He keeps a list of beneficiaries on his computer and has been complying with the Data Protection Act as a Data Controller. Then his trust decides to merge with another one. The new organisation is technically a new Data Controller, but the committee decides not to contact previous beneficiaries of either trust whose records are now in the new combined archive, on the grounds of disproportionate effort. They minute this decision, so that it is on record.

For further examples of the first Data Protection Principle in operation, see Chapter 19.

Chapter 7

Processing sensitive Personal Data

The special categories of 'sensitive' data carry a greater inherent risk than most other data. They therefore have to meet additional, more stringent, conditions before you can process them fairly. Often this means that you will need consent from the Data Subject.

This chapter looks at:

■ The circumstances when you do and do not need consent to process sensitive data

'Sensitive' data, as defined in the Act (see box), is subject to special rules. The definition is quoted here in full and has omissions that may cause surprise. Although details of personal finances, and other data such as age or date of birth, may well be felt by some people to be highly sensitive, it is important to draw the distinction between these personal assessments and the actual requirements of the law.

The first Data Protection Principle states that any Data Controller processing sensitive Personal Data has to meet at least one of the conditions in Schedule 3. This is summarised here, and quoted in full in Appendix B. In addition to the Schedule itself, the Secretary of State has powers to extend the list of conditions. This has been done under Regulations,[22] which are taken into account in the discussion that follows.

---

22 Statutory Instrument 2000 No. 417.

Sensitive Personal Data[23]

. . . is Personal Data consisting of information as to:

(a) the racial or ethnic origin of the Data Subject,

(b) his[24] political opinions,

(c) his religious beliefs or other beliefs of a similar nature,

(d) whether he is a member of a trade union (within the meaning of the Trade Union and Labour Relations (Consolidation) Act 1992),

(e) his physical or mental health or condition,

(f) his sexual life,

(g) the commission or alleged commission by him of any offence, or

(h) any proceedings for any offence committed or alleged to have been committed by him, the disposal of such proceedings or the sentence of any court in such proceedings.

To process sensitive data you have to meet at least one of the conditions. For voluntary organisations, those most likely to apply include the following examples.

- You have the Data Subject's 'explicit' consent.

- You have a legal obligation to process the data in connection with employment.

- It is in the 'vital interests' of the Data Subject or another person, and either consent cannot be obtained or it is reasonable to proceed without it.

- You are processing membership data in a church, trade union or political party, subject to certain restrictions.

- The data has been made public deliberately by the Data Subject.

- You need to process the data in connection with giving legal advice or defending legal rights.

- You need to process the data in connection with medical care and have a medical practitioner's duty of confidentiality.

- You are processing data about ethnic or racial origin, disability or religion in order to monitor equal opportunities.

- You need to process the data in order to provide confidential counselling, advice, support or other services, and either consent cannot be obtained or it is reasonable to proceed without it.

---

23 See paragraph 2 of the Act.

24 UK legislation is not yet written in a gender-neutral way. Where the Act itself is quoted, 'he', 'him' and 'his' apply equally to women.

Other conditions relate to insurance and crime prevention, for example. The intention is clearly that in most cases a Data Controller should aim to meet the **first condition,** which is to have the explicit consent of the Data Subject. 'Explicit' is not defined, and guidance from the Information Commissioner suggests only that explicit consent needs to be clearer and more detailed than the consent which may be sought for processing non-sensitive data (see Chapter 8).

You can process sensitive Personal Data *without* the Data Subject's explicit consent only if one of the other conditions applies. In the rest of this chapter, we will look at these, and circumstances in which they might apply, one by one. If you believe that any of these conditions might apply, consult Appendix B for the full wording of the condition.

Processing sensitive data without consent

The **second condition** provides for processing that is necessary for the purposes of complying with the law in connection with employment. This is a very narrow definition. It is standard employment practice, for example, to hold much more information about an employee's health than is strictly required by law. The Information Commissioner's Code of Practice on employment records does not really resolve this issue. It makes the case that if consent to process the data is made a condition of employment, it may not be valid, as it fails the test of being 'freely given', but the Code then fails to suggest which of the other conditions might make it legitimate to process employee health data without consent. Few employers appear to have addressed this issue, and contractual requirements to consent to the processing of sensitive data are still commonplace.

Can sensitive data be implied? If someone is the contact for the local Sikh gurdwara does that mean I am holding information about their religious beliefs?

A common sense approach is probably required. If the circumstances suggest that the individual definitely falls into a particular category where the data would be sensitive, then treat it as such. Think about whether you actually need the data in question, and whether you can make any disclosures in a less revealing way. (Don't forget, however, that where data has been made deliberately public, the conditions are met.)

In many cases no sensitive data is necessarily implied. People may sign up to receive mailings about a particular medical condition without having it themselves; they may be involved in treating it, for example. This list would therefore not be sensitive.

> **We have a wall chart in our office, showing staff absences. Colour codes indicate the reason for the absence, including 'sick'. Is this OK?**
>
> Quite possibly not. The fact that someone is sick is sensitive Personal Data, and they may not want their colleagues to draw adverse conclusions. (Equally, the work environment may be very supportive and the staff member may be happy for their colleagues to know exactly what is wrong; but that should be the Data Subject's choice.)
>
> An alternative would be to mark them as 'out of the office', so that colleagues know to take messages and so on, but for only the line manager to know whether this is due to illness, a course, a meeting, working from home or waiting in for the gas engineer.

The **third condition** allows processing that is necessary in order to protect the vital interests of the Data Subject *or another person*, in cases where consent cannot be obtained or where it is reasonable to proceed without it. 'Vital interests', in the Information Commissioner's view, again relates to life or death situations only.

> **We want to use the third condition to keep a database of known sex offenders who are deemed unsuitable to work with our vulnerable clients. Is this OK?**
>
> Probably not. The Information Commissioner views 'vital interests' as meaning life or death only, and has also pointed out other potential problems with such a proposal – for example the difficulty in being sure that you have identified people correctly and recorded the details sufficiently accurately. A Criminal Records Bureau check is much more likely to be the appropriate course of action (see Appendix C).

The **fourth condition** allows non-profit organisations with religious, political, trade union or philosophical aims to process sensitive data about their members, or people in regular contact with the organisation, subject to certain safeguards. This is permitted because, by their nature, such organisations will inevitably hold sensitive data. Verbal guidance from the Information Commissioner's staff confirms that 'philosophical' aims do not cover the activities of most charities or voluntary organisations. An equivalent provision for medical self-help groups would be logical, but does not seem to be on the cards.

The **fifth condition** covers sensitive data that the Data Subject has deliberately made public. You would not, for example, need consent to record the political affiliation of someone who had stood as a candidate for a specific party.

The **sixth condition** allows sensitive data to be processed without consent where it is necessary in connection with legal proceedings, obtaining legal advice or establishing, exercising or defending legal rights. While an agency giving legal advice would normally have no problem getting consent from clients, this could allow data about third parties to be held without their consent in connection with a broad range of legal advice work.

The **seventh condition** is very similar to the equivalent condition in Schedule 2, exempting government functions from the need to obtain consent for processing sensitive data, but it lacks the provision for 'functions of a public nature' exercised by others.

The **eighth condition** relates to processing sensitive data where it is necessary for medical purposes, but only where this is done by a health professional or someone who owes an equivalent duty of confidentiality. 'Medical purposes' is defined quite widely, to include care as well as treatment. However, it does not apply to employers seeking medical references from potential employees. The employer would need the Data Subject's consent for this use of their medical records.

The **ninth condition** makes specific provision to permit processing of sensitive data about ethnic or racial origin where this is aimed at promoting equal opportunities. Among the **additional conditions** that have been added by Regulation are ones providing for the use of information on disability or religion for equalities monitoring. In these cases the Regulation states specifically that the information must not be used for making decisions about individuals.

Our equal opportunities monitoring cannot be done anonymously. Do we need consent?

Normally, no. However, if you do not seek consent you *must* make it clear that providing the information is optional, and you *must not* use the information for any purpose other than equal opportunities.

Monitoring on grounds of racial or ethnic origin, disability or religion (which are all sensitive data) are given specific provision, while age, gender or other grounds such as where people live are not sensitive data and you could argue that it is in your legitimate interests. You should be more careful where you are asking about sexuality or criminal record for monitoring purposes, as there is no special provision for these, and they are 'sensitive'.

The other **additional conditions** include one allowing processing of sensitive data for the provision of *confidential* counselling, advice, support or other services, provided that certain safeguards are met. The processing must be in the 'substantial public interest', and it is only permissible if, in addition:

- consent cannot be obtained; or
- it is unreasonable to obtain consent; or
- seeking consent would jeopardise the provision of the service.

This simplifies matters in a number of tricky areas where the Data Subjects may be distressed or otherwise unable to give meaningful consent. It may be more honest to use this condition than to obtain spurious 'consent'. For example, a voluntary organisation providing support to carers might well be able to hold information about the medical condition of the person being cared for without their consent (which may be impossible or unreasonable to obtain). A counselling service should be able to record allegations of abuse without seeking the consent of the alleged abuser.

If relying on this condition, it is important to ensure that you maintain strict confidentiality. This protects the individual from the potential harm that could result if their sensitive data were to end up in the wrong hands.

Summary

To process sensitive Personal Data, you must meet at least one of the following conditions. Your processing must:

- be with the explicit consent of the Data Subject;
- be necessary to meet legal requirements in connection with employment;
- be necessary to protect the vital interests of the Data Subject or another person;
- concern the membership records of certain specified non-profit membership associations;
- involve information deliberately publicised by the Data Subject;
- be in connection with legal advice or protecting legal rights;
- be in connection with a range of government functions;
- be necessary to provide medical care;
- concern equalities monitoring on race/ethnicity, disability or religion;
- be necessary in connection with confidential counselling, advice or support work;
- be in connection with the provision of insurance, or certain other situations.

In most cases there are limitations to the extent to which the conditions may be fulfilled. See Appendix B for the full details.

Examples

1) Louise runs the fundraising department for a small medical charity. Quite often people write in with a donation and mention in the accompanying letter that the reason they are giving the donation is because they themselves have the medical condition in question. Louise would like to keep this information on file for when she writes back in future, and wonders whether the fifth condition in Schedule 3 might apply: has the information been made 'deliberately public' by the Data Subject, or does she need to go back and get explicit consent?

   She telephones the Information Commissioner's Office, where she is told that in its view the letter does not count as being 'public'. So if Louise does want to keep the information she will need to satisfy one of the other conditions. In this case that almost certainly means phoning or writing back to get explicit consent.

2) Maddy is the manager of a carers' support project. Her volunteers visit carers at home, and in the course of their work pick up a lot of information about not just the carer but also the person they are caring for. Some of this information is 'sensitive', such as details about the medical condition of the person being cared for.

   Maddy's approach is twofold. First she has to make sure that she records only information that she genuinely needs. She consults the volunteers and they reach an agreement about the types of information that need to go into the files, both for the organisation's own monitoring and so that volunteers can pass on to each other the information they need in order to provide the services.

   Second, some of this information does relate to the medical condition of the person being cared for and is therefore sensitive Personal Data. The agency workers decide that they are able to guarantee confidentiality and that many of the people being cared for would not be in a position to give consent. They will therefore hold this information under the 'confidential services' condition.

   A colleague of Maddy's, Thomas, faces a slightly different situation. His volunteers are involved in mediation and they sometimes have to visit households where some of the residents have a history of criminal violence. For the safety of the volunteers, Thomas feels it is essential that they are aware of situations like this and, again, that it may not be appropriate to seek consent. He decides to take advice on whether he can use the same argument as Maddy or rely on the third condition, 'protecting vital interests'.

Chapter 8

Data Subject consent

One of the most important questions you have to answer is whether you need consent for the uses you make of people's data.

This chapter looks at:

■ All the questions surrounding consent and how to obtain it

When do I need consent?

Informed consent is a sound basis for a good relationship with your Data Subjects, but it is not mandatory. In the case of Schedule 2 there are six conditions, of which consent is only one, and in Schedule 3 it is one of a score or more. Each of the conditions is of equal value, and you only have to meet one of them in each case.

It is always worth considering whether it is more appropriate to meet one of the other conditions – either because the situation is routine and relatively risk-free or because the process of obtaining genuine consent would be onerous, either for you or for the Data Subject, and you are confident that sufficient safeguards are in place.

Where you are working with adults who cannot give consent, for example, or where you do not feel able to seek consent, you may feel it is more honest to meet one of the conditions for processing without consent, rather than getting a meaningless signature on a piece of paper.

The great advantage of consent, however, is that you are allowing the Data Subject to play a major part in assessing the risk of your intended processing. They are likely to know their situation better than you do; informed consent is, in effect, them saying: 'I have decided that the benefits to me of this transaction outweigh the risks'.

On the other hand, where you are confident that the risk is low, it is often perfectly acceptable to rely on the sixth condition.

The sixth Schedule 2 condition

6 (1) The processing is necessary for the purposes of legitimate interests pursued by the Data Controller or by the third party or parties to whom the data are disclosed, except where the processing is unwarranted in any particular case by reason of prejudice to the rights and freedoms or legitimate interests of the Data Subject.

(2) The Secretary of State may by order specify particular circumstances in which this condition is, or is not, to be taken to be satisfied.

Note that this condition explicitly applies to disclosures as well as to processing for your own purposes. However, you have to be sure that you are not riding rough-shod over the Data Subject's interests, or even putting them at risk. This makes it particularly important to discharge your transparency obligations effectively: if the Data Subject knows fully what is going on, and has either gone ahead with a transaction or not raised any objection to specific aspects of it, you are much more likely to be compliant with the condition, and hence with the first Data Protection Principle.

If you do this you may, in effect, have consent in any case, as we shall see below. Often, the key consideration is not which condition you meet – as you may well meet more than one – but the extent to which you have identified potential risks to your Data Subjects, and given them the information on which they can base their own risk assessment.

What counts as consent?

'Consent' is not defined in the Data Protection Act. Guidance from the Information Commissioner, based on the EU Directive from which the Act is derived, indicates that consent has to be 'freely given, specific and informed'.

The Data Subject must also 'signify' their wishes, which means that, according to the Information Commissioner, there must be some 'active communication' between the parties. Consent can be inferred from something the Data Subject does, but not from something they don't do. In other words, if the Data Subject knows fully what is going to be done with their data and goes ahead with providing it, they can be taken to have consented. However, if you mail people saying 'we'll keep you on our database unless you tell us otherwise', the Information Commissioner's view is that you don't have consent from those who don't reply, because they haven't done anything.

Although the consent must be 'freely given', you are allowed to explain the direct consequences of not consenting. For example, 'Without your national insurance number we can't find out what has happened to your benefits claim.'

The Commissioner is not necessarily right, and his guidance does not have the force of law. There are many instances of commercial companies in particular incorporating consent for the processing of Personal Data into a long list of terms and conditions which are most unlikely to be read, let alone understood, by the majority of customers. The Data Subject has no option but to accept the conditions if they want to do business with the company. While many people would argue that this is not entirely consistent with the Commissioner's guidance, it is common practice and has gone largely unchallenged thus far.

The discussion in this chapter adheres more closely to the Commissioner's line, on the basis that voluntary organisations are more likely to be interested in good practice than in minimal compliance with the Act.

Does consent have to be in writing?

No. Verbal consent is just as valid as written consent. The only issue is whether you feel you need evidence that consent was given. In many cases, you may not feel any need for evidence. Suppose, for example, you have a client in front of you and you ask: 'Is it OK if I pass your details on to organisation X so that it can help you?' When they say 'Yes', you make the phone call, and that's it.

On the other hand, you may feel that it would be safer to have evidence, in case the Data Subject's understanding and yours diverge in future. A signature on a piece of paper is one solution, provided the Data Subject signed in the full knowledge of what they were getting into. Alternatives would include the following.

■ Obtaining verbal consent, then writing to the Data Subject to confirm what you have agreed, and giving them the option to raise any disagreement.
■ Being able to demonstrate that you have consistent procedures for obtaining informed consent, which are regularly checked and monitored.
■ Making an entry in the record at the time to confirm that you have obtained consent. Your data collection forms could be adapted to give a space for this.
■ Making the consent box on screen mandatory with no default: in other words, anyone filling in the form on screen cannot proceed without actively entering yes or no.
■ Asking a sample of clients whether their consent was actively sought and properly explained.

Whatever you decide to do, you must make sure that all your staff and volunteers understand when they need to get clear consent, and know how to do it.

Data obtained from the Data Subject

When you collect information on paper, or on an electronic form, you will often be in a position to provide all the information the Data Subject needs in order to decide whether to give consent. It may be completely obvious from the context who will use the data being collected and what for, for example on a booking form, an order form or an application form, where the name of the organisation collecting the data will be prominent and the purpose clear. You may want to reinforce this by providing a short Data Protection statement ensuring that the Data Subject is in no doubt. If they go ahead and fill in the form, and you are happy that they know exactly what they are letting themselves in for, you can take it that you have their consent.

You may be in the same situation when people give you information face to face or over the phone. If they have initiated the contact – by visiting your agency or phoning you up – they have done something specific and, again provided you are sure that they have all the information they need, you may be able to assume consent. If the contact is trivial you may need to say nothing: they phone up to order a free brochure and you record their address merely so that you can send the brochure out when it is published in two weeks' time. Provided you won't keep the information after that, or use it for something else, they know all they need to know.

In other cases you may need to be more specific, or even to check that you do have their consent. For example, you may need to say, 'Do you mind if we keep your details so that we can let you know if we publish any other material on the same topic?'

When the contact is the beginning of a closer relationship, such as when you take on a new client, you are likely to spend time explaining the arrangements anyway, and can take more time to ensure that they give fully informed consent to your use of their data. It is particularly easy to include consent if you need them to sign something at this stage, agreeing to the service you are providing. You can build consent for your use of their data into the statement they sign.

Data not obtained from the Data Subject

Where you obtain data from a third party you are obviously not in a position to get consent from the Data Subject. Although they may originally have given the organisation or individual that is the source of the data consent to disclose it, this is not the same as giving you consent to use it (because consent must be 'specific'). If you need or want their consent, you have to seek it directly.

Data you hold already

You might be holding information that you obtained a long time ago without seeking consent. Do you need to do anything? It depends on the circumstances.

If the data is used for something that involves the Data Subject doing something, you probably don't need to take any specific action. For example, if they renew their membership annually, the fact that they return their membership renewal is likely to count as consent. Of course, you mustn't use the data for anything they wouldn't expect as a member. You would need to look at the information they were provided with when they originally signed up, or which you had sent them since.

If the data is being kept for historical purposes – old client records, for example – the main requirement is for you to be sure that you are not keeping it for longer than necessary. Provided you are satisfied about this, then it is probably in your legitimate interests to keep the data, and the Data Subject is not being harmed. If so, you do not need to seek consent.

> **We hold information about participants on our training courses, which they supply on the booking form. We also want to collect additional data about them for other purposes: specifically, we would like to take pictures of the participants, as evidence for our funders and to use in next year's courses brochure. Is it enough just to tell people that this is what we do, or do we need their active consent?**
>
> You need to think this through carefully. The closer the additional purpose is to the main one, the less necessary it is to get consent. It could be argued that providing evidence to the funder is inextricably linked to the provision of the training. Any associated risk to the Data Subjects is also low, assuming that the photos are not going to be widely published. In that case, provided you tell people clearly at the time they book (and perhaps remind them at the time you take the photos), you probably don't need to do any more.
>
> If you are going to publish the photos widely, there is a clear risk that at least some people would feel put out to find their picture appearing (and implicitly endorsing your training) without their agreement. Group shots of a large event are unlikely to be a problem, but if you want to use a picture that clearly identifies one or two people, you may decide that it is prudent to get their consent before you use it in something like a brochure or other promotional material.

A more complex area is the type of database where you may need to contact people infrequently, but there is no regular relationship. This could include, for example, a list of people who receive your annual report, or a list of people who you hope may give you money in the future (and who may have given in the past) but who are not currently active donors. If you want their consent, and aim to follow the Information Commissioner's guidance, you cannot just write to say 'tell us if you want to come off the database'. That may be a worthwhile action in its own right, but it does not solve your problem because a non-response would *not count* as consent according to the Commissioner.

The first consideration here is to make sure that everyone on the database knows that you are holding their data and why. If the names are just sitting there and not being used there is a risk that you are holding them longer than necessary. If you are not using the information, why are you holding it? If, however, you decide that you do have a legitimate interest in continuing to hold the data, then you do not necessarily need consent (for example, if you are planning a centenary appeal to all your old members in a few years' time). In any case, it is worth making sure that you contact everyone on the list at some stage to ensure that they know you have the data, and to tell them how to get taken off your database if this is what they want.

'Explicit' consent for sensitive data

When you need explicit consent, you cannot assume that you have it merely from the fact that someone goes ahead with providing information. You need to spell out why you need the data and how you will use it, including any safeguards that you will apply, and any self-imposed restrictions on disclosures (such as not making any disclosure without the Data Subject's consent).

Where the Data Subject is providing information on a paper form and is signing a statement anyway, you can incorporate their consent into the statement. Applicants for a job may be undertaking that the statements they have given on the form are true. New clients may be asking you to take on a particular piece of work, and possibly giving you permission to act for them. Parents may be authorising you to take their children on outings or to administer medicine in emergencies. In any of these cases it is relatively easy to add a sentence to the statement they sign, inviting the person to give explicit consent for any processing of sensitive data.

The same principles could be applied to an electronic form, with appropriate safeguards to verify the identity of the individual.

The most important consideration when you are getting consent for the use of sensitive data is to be explicit about why you want it and how you will use it. For example, the booking forms for your training courses might say: 'Is there anything we can do to help you participate fully in the course? (See brochure for what we can offer.) Any information you give us here will be passed only to the course tutor and/or relevant staff so that they can make appropriate arrangements.' Anyone who then provides you with information about their health, for example, has consented to that use.

> **Does 'explicit' consent have to be in writing?**
>
> No. You may want to get it in writing, so that you can demonstrate that you have provided all the information required. You could have a statement for people to sign, saying, 'I have read the information above about how the centre uses my information, and I am happy for this to happen.' But the important thing is to provide the explicit information before asking for the data.

Consent is not necessarily universal or permanent

The Information Commissioner has expressed the view that the Data Subject may be entitled to consent to some of the things you want to do with their data but at the same time to withhold consent from others. For example, if Data Subjects need to provide information in order to receive a service, they are likely to consent to that. But if you also intend to use the information for other purposes you may need to get consent for these separately. In particular, you may decide to get specific consent for disclosing data to someone else if this is not connected with the main purpose for which the information is being obtained by you.

To be confident that such consent has been 'freely given', it is good practice to provide an opt out from the secondary uses. Your form could say, for example: 'We would also like to pass your details to other organisations offering services you might be interested in. If you do not want us to do this, please tick here [ ]'. Anyone who sends the form back without ticking the box may be taken to have consented to the secondary use.

Don't forget, however, that in many everyday situations you may not need consent at all, if you meet one of the other five conditions.

Data Subjects may also withdraw consent. If you are relying on consent for meeting the fair processing conditions (in Schedule 2) and the Data Subject then decides to withdraw their consent, it would quite possibly be unfair to carry on using the data under one of the other conditions, even if you could genuinely meet one or more of them.

Summary

- Consent is not mandatory; in some situations it is highly appropriate to seek consent, in others it may not be.
- Consent to use Personal Data must be freely given, specific and informed.
- Consent need not be in writing.
- Consent can normally be implied from something the Data Subject does, but not from anything they fail to do.
- For 'explicit' consent to process sensitive data, you must explain carefully why you need the information and what you will do with it.

Examples

1) Miles runs a membership organisation. Every year members get a letter asking them to renew their subscription. He decides to include in the letter a statement that members' data will be used only for administering member activities and benefits. He reasons that if members go ahead and send the form back, they have consented to this use of their data.

   However, someone on the committee then proposes publishing a county-by-county list of members, so that they can get in touch with each other. Before the plan is put into action, Miles points out that this is a new venture; people may not have realised that it would be one of the member services to be undertaken, so they cannot be said to have consented to it.

   The whole project is shelved until members can be asked, both in principle at the AGM and individually, whether they want their details made public in this way.

2) Sue's advice agency has a strict confidentiality policy. When new clients sign up, they are always told that there are a very few circumstances when the centre is legally obliged to break confidentiality, but that otherwise no disclosures will be made without their consent. Whenever the client visits the centre, staff are careful to ask for consent before making any referrals. However, if they need to consult specialist colleagues about a case they do not seek consent if the consultation can take place without identifying the client, since this does not involve disclosing Personal Data and is not a breach of confidentiality.

Chapter 9

Data quality

The third and fourth Data Protection Principles cover data quality. You must be able to justify why you are holding any particular data, and it must be fit for purpose. Inaccurate or poor-quality data could cause harm to your Data Subjects.

This chapter:

- Examines the requirements for data quality
- Proposes an approach to record-keeping

Taken together, the third and fourth Principles say that your data must be:

- **adequate**: you must have sufficient data to support any decisions or actions you are taking in respect of the Data Subject. If you don't have enough, you may end up guessing – with a clear risk of guessing wrongly and ending up making the wrong decision or taking the wrong action;

- **relevant**: you must be able to show that the information you are holding relates to the purpose you are holding it for. (Note that the requirement is for it to be 'relevant'; in this respect the legislation does not impose the stricter test of it being 'necessary'.);

- **not excessive**: you must not record more information than you need. If you can make your decision or take your action confidently with a smaller amount of information, you must not collect additional information, even if you could argue that it does relate to your purpose(s);

- **accurate**: the phrasing of the Principle allows no leeway, your data *must* be accurate;

- **where necessary, kept up to date**: this will depend on the purpose you are holding the data for. Clearly the address in your accounting system of someone who paid you money last year doesn't need to be updated if they move (unless they make another payment), but the address of a newsletter subscriber does have to be changed as soon as you are told.

The third Data Protection Principle

Personal Data shall be adequate, relevant and not excessive in relation to the purpose or purposes for which they are processed.

The fourth Data Protection Principle

Personal Data shall be accurate and, where necessary, kept up to date.

Clearly it is not possible in practice for all your data to be completely accurate, because people frequently change their address and other details, and may neglect to tell you. However, there are many ways in which you could cause harm if your data quality was not up to scratch, as the following examples illustrate.

■ Inaccurate financial information could lead to you paying someone the wrong amount or failing to pay them at all. The mistake can almost always be put right eventually, but meanwhile the person is out of pocket and may be put to considerable inconvenience – especially if they were relying on your payment to settle their bills.

■ Inaccurate or insufficient information about a person's qualifications and career history could lead to them not getting a job they were suitable for – or getting a job they were not suitable for.

■ Inaccurate or insufficient information about a person's medical condition, allergy or disability could lead to you putting them in a risky, even life-threatening, situation.

You have a responsibility, therefore, in four main areas:

■ to identify situations where poor-quality data would pose a particular risk, and to ensure that in those situations you pay special attention to checking your information as far as possible before relying on it;

■ to provide your staff with guidance and training in how to keep good records, especially when they have a lot of discretion about what to record and how to record it (in free-text areas of a database, or in paper file notes, for example);

■ to have sound procedures for updating your records when you become aware that information has changed;

■ to have routine procedures for inviting Data Subjects to check and update the information you are holding at appropriate intervals.

What happens if someone deliberately gives me the wrong information? Suppose my client doesn't like the idea of being 78 and tells me they are 68.

It depends on the situation. It may not matter much – if your data is being aggregated for monitoring purposes only, for example – so you could ignore the problem. (But if it doesn't matter *at all*, there is the question of why you are collecting the information in the first place.)

However, it could matter a lot – for instance if you are advising clients on age-related benefits. In this case, you should not assume that your Data Subject understands why you are asking the question. To fulfil your responsibility for data to be accurate, you would need to make sufficient effort to ensure that you have explained why you are asking, and why it matters. If the Data Subject still insists on giving you inaccurate information, you may have to accept that. However, if the data is really critical you could try to verify it in some other way – by asking to see an official document which shows the Data Subject's age or date of birth, for example.

A common problem in many voluntary organisations, especially as they grow, is that information about the same person is held in many different places – perhaps on a membership database and a fundraising database, and in a spreadsheet holding the details of people who are interested in a particular project, and as e-mails in the e-mail system. This, of course, poses difficulties when the person's details change. They may inform one part of the organisation – by asking the membership section to change the address their newsletter is sent to, for example – and assume, quite reasonably, that they have therefore told 'the organisation'. Your challenge is to ensure that everyone else who holds information about that person finds out about the change of address.

There are several options, none of them wholly satisfactory. The most drastic is for the organisation to invest in a central contact management database, so that data on each Data Subject is held in one place only, and accessed by all staff who have dealings with that person. This is usually an expensive and time consuming undertaking, and is very unlikely to be justifiable purely from a Data Protection perspective. However, if the organisation is considering taking this course of action for the other benefits it brings – more flexibility, better relationships with members and contacts, better management information, and so on – it does provide an excellent opportunity to build in support for good Data Protection practice.

In the absence of a central system, it still makes sense to reduce the number of places that information about the same person is held, perhaps by encouraging staff to share data sets when they can, and in particular to delete data sets that are no longer actively needed.

A different approach is to have a register of all the data sets in the organisation and send all changes of details to the person who administers this register. They then have the task of circulating the change to all who may need to update their records.

Does this all mean that I can never write down an opinion or an assumption?

No it doesn't. If it is relevant and not excessive, you can record the information. You may feel that you have no option; without that information the record might be inadequate. What is important is *how* you record the information.

The key points are to:

- check your facts where possible, so as to avoid the need to rely on an opinion or assumption if possible. It may be appropriate to check with the individual, or a more expert colleague, or via authoritative documents;
- quote the evidence on which opinions are based. You should record what has been observed, or what has occurred, and the concern that this raises, rather than just the concern;
- clarify that you are recording an opinion or assumption, so that others using the record know how to respond;
- indicate who has made the entry, so that other members of staff can refer back to them if appropriate.

As well as ensuring that you update your records properly when you are informed of a change, you should consider having a programme for contacting your Data Subjects at appropriate intervals and asking them to check that you still have the correct data.

Where you have membership which has to be renewed periodically, it is often convenient to send out a copy of the data you hold, and ask the member to correct any inaccuracies at the same time as renewing their membership. Increasingly, this can be done online, with members given direct access to an electronic version of their record.

Staff could be invited to check their basic personnel record at the time of their annual appraisal or, again, given online access to the relevant parts of your personnel system.

Where you do not have such an obvious opportunity to review your data, it is still worth contacting Data Subjects at appropriate intervals to ensure that your data is still accurate and up to date.

People who have died

People are no longer Data Subjects after they have died – mainly because they are no longer in a position to be compensated for any harm caused by mishandling their data. However, that is no excuse for failing to respond properly when you are informed that one of your Data Subjects has died.

It may be appropriate to retain the records for some time – for example if the person was a client or a staff member. What you must do, however, is ensure that the record is marked so that it cannot be used inappropriately.

This is particularly important with members, supporters and customers. You are likely to contact these people regularly, and it is very poor practice to risk upsetting their relatives by continuing to mail – or even worse phone – after they have died.

You cannot, of course, take any action until you know that the death has occurred. One option with mailing lists may be provided in the Supply of Information (Register of Deaths) Regulations 2007. This sets up a scheme whereby organisations can pay to be sent weekly lists of all UK registered deaths. At the time of writing the use is limited to 'the prevention, detection, investigation or prosecution of offences', and is specifically aimed at preventing identity theft. However, the Regulations provide that data on deaths 'may' be provided to 'any person or body undertaking list cleaning as defined in these regulations'. This seems potentially to open the way to the data being available for a wider range of purposes in future.

Equally importantly, when you *do* become aware that someone has died, you must have systems in place to ensure that every record you have of that person is suitably amended.

Summary

- All your data must, in principle, be adequate, relevant and not excessive, accurate and, where necessary, kept up to date.
- Poor-quality data could lead to serious harm for your Data Subjects.
- Your systems and procedures should facilitate the keeping of good-quality data.
- You should be careful to record deaths among your Data Subjects appropriately, so that you do not risk trying to contact them in future.

Examples

1) Caroline finds that Wendy, a member of her staff, has made an assumption about a client's medical condition and written it down in their file in such a way that it appears as a fact. It turns out to be incorrect, but meanwhile decisions about the client have been influenced by the wrong information. This is clearly a very serious breach, and could have led to the client being put at serious risk.

   Caroline decides to review her guidance to staff on how to complete case files, and to review all Wendy's case notes for six months, to make sure that she doesn't repeat the mistake.

2) Anwar has organised a training event. At the last minute the leader falls ill and Anwar has to cancel it. He tries to phone all the participants to tell them but one person, Don, has not given a number and still turns up for the event. Don says that if he had known Anwar might want to contact him urgently he would

have given his mobile number on the booking form. He is annoyed at the wasted journey and asks for his travel costs to be repaid.

Anwar feels that Don is trying it on a bit, but when he looks back at the booking form he sees that it didn't explain why the phone number was being asked for. Anwar accepts that his responsibility for 'adequate' data might extend to asking more precise questions, so he pays up as a gesture of goodwill.

3) Peter is working with a group of his organisation's members to prepare a presentation to an awards ceremony. One of the members of the group phones the organisation to say that she has changed her phone number. The receptionist passes the message on to membership. However, Peter never finds out about the change of number. When he tries to contact the member to invite her to the event he can't get hold of her in time, and she is very disappointed to miss out.

At the next team meeting, Peter suggests that the organisation should think about how this might be prevented in the future, but in the meantime the receptionists are told always to ask members what activities they are involved in, to make it more likely that any changes in their contact details can be forwarded to the right people.

Chapter 10

How long should data be kept?

The fifth Data Protection Principle says that data must not be held longer than 'necessary', but many people find it hard to assess what this means. There are also exemptions which apply to archives and historical material.

This chapter covers:

- The issues that apply to retention of archives
- The use of records for historical or statistical purposes

The fifth Data Protection Principle

Personal Data processed for any purpose or purposes shall not be kept for longer than is necessary for that purpose or those purposes.

There is no simple rule for deciding when to destroy, erase or archive data. Each situation is different, depending on what is necessary for the purpose(s) for which you hold the data. The questions you may wish to ask include the following examples.

- Is there a legal time limit for holding this data? For example, some records relating to occupational health now have to be held for 40 years.
- Might you need the information in order to answer a legal claim – for negligence, breach of contract or discrimination, for example? In many cases there is a limit of six years within which a claim may be made, but in other cases the time limit is much shorter: an unsuccessful candidate for a job can only bring a claim of discrimination for up to three months (although many practitioners recommend keeping information on employment selection for about six months). In a few

specific cases the limit for making a negligence claim may in practice be longer than six years.[25]

- Do you have specific advice from professionals? For instance, your indemnity insurer may want you to keep detailed client records for as long as a negligence claim might be valid.

- Has the reason for holding the data changed? When a member of staff leaves, it might be the appropriate time to reduce their file to those items you must archive long term or permanently.

- Do you know for a fact that the information is out of date? If mail is returned, you would have a hard job to justify keeping an address that you know is wrong.

- Is the data used according to a routine rhythm? If you mail people to ask for money twice a year, you may want to set a specific number of non-responses after which you will assume that they have lost interest.

- Can you confidently describe the next time you are going to use the data? If not, it may have outstayed its welcome. Keeping information 'just in case' is not only a waste of your storage space; it is unlikely to be satisfactory Data Protection practice.

A good rule of thumb is to try to imagine any circumstance in which you might be asked to produce the data. If not having the data would matter, then there is clear justification for keeping it. If there is no possibility of being asked for it, or if being unable to produce it wouldn't matter, then there is a strong case for erasing or destroying it.

You should also consider the question of how much the Data Subject knows about your retention policy. If you tell job applicants at the time they apply that their details will be held in case a suitable vacancy comes up in the future, then you are far less likely to be contravening the Principle than if you leave them with the impression that you are only concerned with the single current vacancy.

When the time does come to destroy material, remember that erasure or destruction is still 'processing', so it must still comply with the Principles, including fairness and security. Where you hold highly confidential data you may want to think about using a program to make it irrecoverable from your computer or disk, or about secure destruction methods such as shredding. What you do not want is to throw material away, only for it to turn up blowing around in the street outside your office.

See the Resources section for a selection of suggested guidance notes on retention periods.

---

25 The House of Lords ruled in 2008, for example, that in some abuse cases the limit is in effect indefinite, although the facts of that specific case mean that this does not necessarily apply to other cases.

Research, history and statistics

Even when you have finished using data for its original purpose, if you have a valid reason for keeping it, you do not necessarily have to dispose of it. There is an exemption allowing data to be processed for research, history and statistics, even if this was not the original reason for its collection. Under this exemption the data may be kept indefinitely and may be used regardless of the purpose(s) it was originally obtained for, provided that:

- the processing does not support actions or decisions relating to specific individuals; *and*
- the processing does not cause anyone substantial damage or distress.

You may decide that your archives are of such potential interest in the future – perhaps to researchers, or even to your Data Subjects if you hold information about key events in their lives – that you can easily justify keeping them. It might even be fairer to the Data Subject to keep the information. You should, however, be careful to distinguish between 'live' information and 'historical' archives, and ensure that access to the historical material is suitably restricted.

Statistical material, of course, once individual Data Subjects are no longer identifiable, is not subject to Data Protection restrictions on disclosure, because it has ceased to be Personal Data. If there is no reason to keep the material in such a way that the Data Subject is still identifiable, you may find it more appropriate to convert it into an anonymous form.

Summary

- You cannot continue to keep data without a good reason.
- Take advice on appropriate retention periods from relevant professionals where possible.
- Otherwise, make your own judgement, based on whether you can foresee any point in the future when you would genuinely need the information.
- If you want to keep information longer than the Data Subject might expect, make sure you let them know.
- There are exemptions allowing material to be held indefinitely for research or historical purposes, subject to certain conditions, even if this was not the original purpose.

Chapter 11

Data Subjects' rights

The 1998 Act contains important rights for Data Subjects. Individuals can prevent Data Controllers using their data in certain ways, either by withholding consent or by exercising specific rights.

This chapter:

- Presents a summary of the main Data Subject rights. Key ones are dealt with in more detail in separate chapters, as indicated below

The Principles remind the Data Controller that individual Data Subjects have significant rights under the Act.

The sixth Data Protection Principle

Personal Data shall be processed in accordance with the rights of data subjects under this Act.

In summary, the Data Subjects' rights include the rights to:

- receive specific information (see Chapters 6 and 19);
- opt out of all direct marketing and specific types of marketing by electronic means (see Chapter 12);
- restrict automated decision making (see overleaf);
- prevent processing that causes harm to the Data Subject (see overleaf);
- apply for Subject Access (see Chapter 13);
- ask the Information Commissioner to make an 'Assessment' of whether an organisation or person is complying with the Act (see Chapter 22);
- have inaccurate information corrected (see overleaf);
- receive compensation for harm caused by a Data Protection breach (see page 73).

Automated decision making

The Data Subject has rights in relation to automated decision-making processes, such as:

- credit scoring – if information is fed in and the decision on whether to grant someone credit is made entirely automatically;
- CV assessment – where a CV that is received electronically might be scanned automatically and rejected if the person is 'too old';
- automatically matching people as they pass in front of a CCTV camera against a file of photographs, to identify people who have been barred from the premises.

Since very few voluntary organisations have systems that make completely automatic decisions, these rights are described here only in brief. Voluntary organisations might be able to help their clients to make use of these rights, and so need to be aware of them.

As a Data Subject you have the right to 'require' (11.(1) in the Act) a Data Controller, in writing, not to make any decisions about you entirely automatically.

If you have not done this, decisions may be made automatically, but you have the right to know 'as soon as reasonably practicable' that this is happening. You then have the right to ask for the decision to be reconsidered manually within 21 days. You can go to court to enforce these rights if the Data Controller does not comply with them.

In brief, these rules do not apply if:

- the automatic decision is taken in connection with a legal responsibility or a contract involving you; and
- the effect of the decision is to grant your request or, if it is not granted, your interests are safeguarded in some other way (for example by allowing you to 'make representations').

What this means is that if, for example, you are turned down for credit, or a job, and the decision is made completely automatically, you must be told this and have the right for the decision to be reconsidered. But if you are given the credit you want, you don't have to be told. And if the final decision on whether to shortlist you for the job is checked by a person, you also have no rights to be told or to object.

Processing that harms the Data Subject

The Data Subject has the right to 'require' the Data Controller, in writing, to stop processing their Personal Data in ways that harm the Data Subject. Harm is defined as 'substantial damage or substantial distress' that is 'unwarranted'.

This right is available only if the Data Controller is relying on the fifth or sixth fair processing condition in Schedule 2: the official functions and the 'legitimate interests' of the Data Controller (see Conditions for fair processing in Chapter 6). If the processing is in connection with a contract, for example, the Data Subject cannot prevent it.

If the right to stop processing is exercised, the Data Controller must reply in writing within 21 days, either agreeing to stop or saying why they don't think they should. The Data Subject can take the Data Controller to court if they don't think they have complied properly.

Surveillance

A topic that has grown in importance since the first Data Protection Act was passed in 1984 (with its Orwellian overtones) is the relationship between Data Protection and surveillance. With Britain having the most intensive use of CCTV in the world, and moves to increase the amount of data being forcibly collected or disclosed to government, the 'surveillance society' is a concern for many people. Records of Internet use and data on air passengers have been the subject of intense debate, both at the European and national level.

All surveillance has to comply with Data Protection, but the individual has very few rights to prevent it, at least when it is carried out by public authorities. Its legitimacy does not normally rest on consent, but on specific legal powers. While the debate over surveillance is not one this book can enter into, it is a topic that is likely to affect voluntary organisations – and their clients – increasingly over the coming years.

Legal remedies

Many Data Protection problems will be resolved directly with the Data Controller or through the intervention, formally or informally, of the Information Commissioner. For most Data Subjects court action will be a last resort. This section is therefore a very brief summary.

A Data Subject may use the court to enforce rights within the Act, such as those described immediately above and the right of Subject Access (see Chapter 13).

Someone who has suffered 'damage' by a contravention of the Act can take the Data Controller to court for compensation for the harm done (and may also claim for associated distress).

The court may order the Data Controller to 'rectify, block, erase or destroy' inaccurate data. This applies even if the mistake was made by someone else who provided the data. Alternatively the court may order the Data Controller to add a statement to the record rebutting the inaccuracy. The court may also order the Data Controller to notify anyone to whom they have disclosed the inaccurate information, if this is 'reasonably practicable'.

Chapter 12

Restrictions on fundraising and direct marketing

Data Subjects have the right to prevent you from contacting them with a wide range of unsolicited material, but there is considerable variation in the way organisations respond to this provision. When you assist others with their marketing – through exchange of mailing lists, for example – there are further points to consider.

This chapter:

- Looks in detail at the requirements of the Act in respect of Data Subjects and unsolicited material
- Covers the related Privacy and Electronic Communications (EC Directive) Regulations 2003

For the first time in the UK, the Act gave individuals the right to prevent the use of their data for direct marketing. In this context 'direct marketing' must be taken to include much charity fundraising, as well as many other unsolicited approaches to Data Subjects. Although the onus is on the Data Subject to exercise this right, 'fairness' in processing is likely to require the provision of more information about how data is to be used, as well as the use of opt-out boxes on many leaflets and forms.

This is a significant right, and enables people to stem, or at least reduce, the flow of 'junk mail' and unwanted electronic (phone and e-mail) contact where they wish to.

Don't forget that you can only use people's data for direct marketing if they have been informed that this is one of the purposes for which you use it.

What is direct marketing?

The definition of direct marketing in the Act is broad. It is the '[unsolicited] communication (by whatever means) of any advertising or marketing material which is directed to particular individuals'. At its narrowest this will cover the marketing of goods or publications, distribution of a mail order catalogue, or promotion of services such as training or other events. The Information Commissioner and many practitioners, however, interpret the definition far more broadly. It is generally accepted that any type of fundraising is covered. More controversially, the definition probably also includes a wide range of other activities which are designed in some way to promote the organisation, yet which also benefit the Data Subject.

In the commercial context this makes sense. Few commercial organisations would bother making unsolicited contact with Data Subjects unless there was ultimately something in it for the organisation. Voluntary organisations, however, are much more likely to act altruistically – sending out information which is wholly for the Data Subject's benefit, for example – or where the benefit to the organisation is marginal compared with the benefit to the Data Subject.

At the time of writing, there has been no case law which might clarify the definition. Onerous though it may seem in some instances, the most cautious approach is to class any unsolicited contact as direct marketing unless it clearly has no spin-off benefit for the Data Controller.

A lot of the time our fundraising department doesn't ask people for money, it just sends people information in order to build and develop a relationship with them. This doesn't count as marketing, does it?

The reason why marketing receives special treatment in the Data Protection Act is because many people do regard a lot of the material they receive as junk mail and would prefer not to receive it. Best practice, and the safest option, is to regard anything that is sent on your initiative as marketing, even if it doesn't ask for money or support, unless the information it contains is clearly for the direct benefit of the recipient and has no significant spin-off benefit for you. However, if you find this approach too restrictive, there are many areas around the fringes of marketing where you could probably make the opposite case. You do have to consider, though, the recipient's likely response if you send them material after they have asked not to receive marketing.

If the law were to accept this approach, direct marketing would include, for example:

- sending a book of raffle tickets to buy or sell;
- inviting someone to a free event designed to promote the organisation;
- sending out membership reminders, asking people to renew their membership;
- asking a previous donor to sign up to Gift Aid.

While there may be some doubt over the types of content which count as marketing, there is no doubt over the form it takes: restrictions on direct marketing apply to *any* form of contact, including (but not limited to) mail, phone calls, faxes, e-mail and text messages.

The material has to be advertising or marketing and directed to the individual. Therefore, it is hard to see how the restrictions would apply to:

- material purely for information, for example an update to a previous information request;
- a flyer or brochure inserted in every copy of a magazine or other mailing;
- advertisements within publications or on posters;
- marketing material sent to an organisation, even via a contact person, provided you are asking the organisation to respond, not the individual.

There are those, however, who would argue that if it is physically possible to send a newsletter out without its marketing content, then the option to opt out should be available. Many organisations face this issue, for example when the marketing material – such as a Christmas card catalogue or a book of raffle tickets – is being sent out with a membership mailing, but on behalf of another part of the organisation, or even a separate but linked trading company.

The right to opt out of direct marketing

The Act provides that the Data Subject may 'require' the Data Controller in writing not to use their data for direct marketing. However, you cannot leave it entirely up to the Data Subject to take the initiative, because of your responsibility to be 'fair' when obtaining information.

If you are obtaining the information directly from the Data Subject, in order to be fair you should in most cases give them the opportunity to opt out there and then, preferably through having a box to tick if they don't want future contact (an 'opt-out box'). It is much less likely to be fair if you tell them that they have to send in a form or write to a separate address in order to opt out.

Our fundraising manager doesn't want to frighten people off by putting opt-out boxes on the membership form. He wants to give the information in a follow-up letter and leave it up to the Data Subject to get in touch. Is this OK?

Probably, though it may not be best practice. You have to put as few obstacles in people's way as possible. European Directive 95/46/EC says that the Data Subject has the right to object 'free of charge' to direct marketing (though this requirement does not appear in the UK legislation). If the person is filling in a form and could be given the option of ticking a box, it is arguably not 'free of charge' to make them contact you separately in an alternative way. If you really don't want to put the opt-out box on your data capture forms, you should at least think of giving them a freepost card to return or a freephone number to call.

If you obtain the information from elsewhere (for example when you swap lists with another organisation), you need to make it clear as soon as you use the information – in most cases at your first contact with the Data Subjects – that you are using it for direct marketing. You must also tell them clearly that they can opt out, and make this as easy as possible for them. Again, anything that puts unnecessary obstacles in their way (such as a premium rate opt-out phone number) could well be unfair.

When someone opts out this applies only where the material is unsolicited. If you advertise something in your newsletter and someone phones up to ask for more information, you can send a brochure even if they are marked on your database for 'no direct marketing'.

Approaching someone who has given money in the past to ask for another donation counts as unsolicited direct marketing, but following up a specific transaction is not. If someone sends a donation but forgets to sign their donation cheque, there is nothing to stop you getting back to them on that specific point, even if they have opted out of direct marketing.

When people have participated in an event, we assume that they will be interested in the same event again next year. Do we have to tell them we're going to contact them again, and give them an opt-out?

You should certainly make them aware that you will be retaining their details for the future. Technically you do not have to offer an opt-out, though it is good practice to do so. If you have not given them an opt-out box to tick, but have explained to them how you will be using their data, then it would be up to them to 'require' you not to market in future. This may not apply to marketing by e-mail (see page 80).

The importance of the marketing opt-out can be seen in relation to the electoral roll. There is a legal requirement to be on the electoral roll and it must be made public – usually by being available for consultation in libraries. Local authorities can recoup part of their costs by making the electoral roll available electronically to commercial organisations, which then use it for purposes such as credit checking and direct marketing.

The Representation of the People Act 2000 took account of Data Protection by making provision for electors to opt out of the disclosure of their details for these additional purposes, but the government did not implement the relevant section in time for the 2001 compilation of the electoral roll. One local authority was taken to court[26] as a result of not having offered the opt-out, and lost.

Since December 2002, therefore, there have been two versions of the electoral roll: the full register, which is used for electoral, crime prevention and other limited purposes, such as credit checking. The edited register is available for sale to anyone. Unfortunately for those who might want to reduce 'junk mail', the wording for the opt-out box which electors have to tick if they do not want their details made available for marketing is confusing, so this provision has probably had less impact than it might otherwise have done.

Trading companies, list swaps and marketing on behalf of other organisations

Where a charity has a linked trading company there are, in effect, two Data Controllers. They may operate independently or they may, if they have access to a common database, be joint Data Controllers of the same data. Either way, it is necessary for each Data Controller to ensure that the Data Subject knows that their data is going to be used by the other.

Many voluntary organisations also exchange data for marketing purposes, by swapping lists, by carrying out reciprocal mailings or by enclosing other organisations' marketing material in with their own mailings.

'Trading/sharing in personal information' is a standard purpose, described by the Information Commissioner as 'the sale, hire, exchange or disclosure of Personal Data to third parties in return for goods/services/benefit'. This means that any kind of list swap is likely to be covered *even if you send out material on behalf of the other organisation and do not actually disclose the data itself to them*. Where the other party is your own trading company, there is still a strong possibility that you are trading in Personal Data because 'you' are giving 'them' data in return for the funds 'they' raise.

You must therefore consider whether to include 'Trading/sharing in personal information' as one of the purposes in your notification (see Chapter 21); it is not an 'exempt' purpose. More importantly, you must ensure that your Data Subjects are made aware that their data will be passed to another Data Controller for marketing purposes, *and* you must explain how they can opt out of this use.

Wherever possible this should be done at the time you obtain information from your Data Subjects, and preferably with an opt-out box on the form, along the lines of 'We would also like to send you material from our trading company' or 'From time to time

---

26 The 'Robertson' case. R v City of Wakefield Metropolitan Council and another *ex parte* Robertson (16 November 2001).

we will send material from (or 'we will pass your name to') other organisations we believe you will be interested in', and in each case finishing off with 'If you do not want us to do this, please tick this box [ ]'.

Our sponsored events people want to pass on the names of participants to our fundraising department. Can they do this?

If the transfer is within one Data Controller, then it depends on what you told people you would do with their data. Provided the event sign-up form was clear that the data might be used for future marketing, and they are able to opt out, then it doesn't matter which part of the organisation they hear from.

The Privacy and Electronic Communications (EC Directive) Regulations 2003

A separate piece of legislation, the Privacy and Electronic Communications (EC Directive) Regulations 2003,[27] often abbreviated to PECR, gives additional rights with respect to marketing carried out by telephone, fax, e-mail, text message and any other electronic medium. These Regulations are also enforced by the Information Commissioner.

The Regulations allow an individual[28] telephone subscriber to 'notify' a caller that they don't want any further telemarketing calls from them. This 'notification' does not have to be in writing. Essentially, you can tell anyone who rings with a marketing call, 'Don't call again', and that should be sufficient. The definition of marketing is essentially the same as in the Data Protection Act.

The Regulations also provide the statutory basis for the Telephone Preference Service (TPS).[29] Any individual subscriber can (in theory) prevent all unwanted marketing calls by registering their phone number. Before any person or organisation makes a marketing call they must check the number they intend to ring against the register. If the number is on the register, direct marketing calls must not be made to it. It doesn't matter whether the number is from your own database, from someone else's list, from the phone book or dialled at random.

A phone number can be added to the register by phone or on the TPS website. The number to call, at the time of writing, is 0845 070 0707. Information is also available from the operator and is given near the front of up-to-date telephone directories.

---

27 SI 2003 No. 2426, subsequently amended by SI 2004 No. 1039.
28 'Individual' in this connection includes not only phone lines held in the name of individuals, but also those held in the name of unincorporated voluntary organisations and businesses, such as law firms, accountancy firms, surveyors, etc.
29 Operated under contract by the Direct Marketing Association.

Business lines can also be placed on the TPS register, but the request must be made in writing (by mail or on the website), so that you can confirm that you are authorised to take this action. A business registration must be renewed annually.

The TPS service can be used for mobile phones, but only applies to voice calls, not text messages.

The TPS service is very popular and largely successful, even though the service cannot prevent marketing calls made from overseas. By September 2007, 14.7 million numbers were registered, with 200,000 having been added that July.

If you wish to make marketing calls, the register can be checked in a number of ways. Users who make large numbers of calls can subscribe to the national register, or subsets of it, in electronic format for a fee. (See Further information at the end of the book for details.) There are also low-volume options, including a premium-rate phone line which allows individual numbers to be checked one at a time. Alternatively, if you are using the services of a bureau to make calls for you, it should be able to check your list of numbers as part of the service, or you could use the services of a specialist 'list cleanser'.

The only way to make marketing calls without checking the register is if you already have permission for this from the person you are calling. Such consent for marketing calls continues to apply, even if the subscriber subsequently puts their number on the register. It may be worth pointing this out to people when seeking their consent for telemarketing. Note also that the TPS applies to the line, not the individual. It does not appear to be possible for one member of a family to agree to receiving calls if the others do not want them.

In a few, well-defined cases, it may be possible to argue for a slight relaxation in these rules. For example, in 2007 a major charity argued successfully with the Information Commissioner that it would be acceptable to call long-standing regular donors, even if their numbers were on the TPS register and no consent had been obtained. This was part of a one-off campaign to transfer donors by standing order to direct debit. Donors were asked at the outset of the call whether they were happy to accept the call, and at the end of the call whether they were happy to be contacted by phone in future.[30]

The Regulations also forbid sending unsolicited faxes to individuals' lines unless they have given permission in advance. Businesses can prevent unwanted marketing faxes by registering with the Fax Preference Service (on 0845 070 0702) which operates on similar lines to the TPS.

The Regulations also apply to e-mail marketing to individuals, but in a very limited way. E-mail and text message marketing is permitted if the recipient is an existing

---

30 *Third Sector*, 5 October 2007.

customer and the marketing relates to similar goods or services being offered by the same organisation, provided each text or e-mail explains to the recipient how to unsubscribe from future such marketing. E-mail and text message marketing to anyone else is prohibited unless they have given specific prior consent.

However, the rights belong to the subscriber, not to the individual receiving the e-mail. A significant effect of this is that e-mail marketing to private individuals at work e-mail addresses is not restricted. However, unincorporated associations are, for these purposes, individuals and should, therefore, benefit from the restrictions. In some circumstances it is likely to be hard for a marketing company reliably to make this distinction.

All advertising or marketing e-mails must contain clear instructions on a simple procedure to opt out of receiving them in future.

Other than this, normal restrictions on marketing apply: if someone has required you not to market to them, then this includes marketing by e-mail or other electronic means.

Communications by e-mail and the web are also covered in Chapter 18.

Good practice

Marketing is an area that can provoke strong feelings. The Fundraising Standards Board reported in May 2008 that 31% of the 8,434 complaints it received in the year to February 2008 were about direct mail, and 22% were about Data Protection.[31]

Some would argue that the need for funds is so great that fundraisers should not allow themselves to be restricted by anything more than bare compliance with the law. Others point to the popularity of the TPS, and to the level of complaints about 'junk mail', and argue that a better result will be achieved in the long term by working for greater public acceptance – for example by moving towards 'permission-based marketing'.

For sources of guidance on good fundraising practice see Further information at the end of the book.

Practical implications

It is important that, if you make any use of direct marketing, your system is able to record who has consented or objected to what. The system must be reliably able to 'suppress' any individual's details if they have opted out. While a manual system may suffice for small numbers, an automatic system is likely to be more accurate.

---

31 Reported in *Third Sector*, 14 May 2008.

It is up to you whether you allow nuances in opting out. There is nothing to prevent you giving people the choice to receive, for example, information about membership benefits but not a trading catalogue, or invitations to participate in sponsored events but not raffle tickets. The basic minimum, however, is a blanket 'yes' or 'no' to all marketing material.

When someone does opt out, deleting them altogether from your database may be unwise. If you ever came across their name again, you would have no record that they had exercised their direct marketing opt-out and you may inadvertently end up marketing to them again, against their wishes.

You should also ensure that if you transfer data to other organisations for marketing purposes, either you exclude anyone who has opted out of direct marketing, or you include their opt-out status with the information transferred. If you obtain marketing databases from other organisations you need guarantees that they have excluded (or marked) those who have opted out of direct marketing. Although this is not sufficient to ensure that your marketing is compliant with the Act, such a guarantee will give you recourse if you inadvertently send direct marketing to someone who has opted out.

Finally, it is important that all your staff and volunteers who may be in contact with Data Subjects understand the full implications of these rights. There must be a clear procedure for acting on the wishes of anyone who says 'Stop sending me this stuff' or 'Stop phoning me'.

Summary

Who	Can prevent	Who to	How	Under
Data Subject	All unsolicited direct marketing from one organisation	Data Controller	'Require in writing'	Data Protection Act 1998
Domestic phone subscriber	Unsolicited telephone marketing from one organisation	Caller or their organisation	'Notify'	Privacy etc. Regulations 2003
Domestic phone subscriber	Unsolicited telephone marketing from any organisation	Telephone Preference Service	Website or 0845 070 0707	Privacy etc. Regulations 2003
Business phone subscriber	Unsolicited telephone marketing from any organisation	Telephone Preference Service	Website or written application	Privacy etc. Regulations amendment 2004
Business fax subscriber	Unsolicited fax marketing from any organisation	Fax Preference Service	Website or 0845 070 0702	Privacy etc. Regulations 2003
Individual e-mail subscriber	Unsolicited e-mails except when existing customer and product/ service is similar	Not required – automatic		Privacy etc. Regulations 2003

Data Protection

Examples

Barbara is the fundraiser for a small charity. Someone sends a donation out of the blue in response to an article in the local paper. Barbara decides that she might want to ask them for more money in future, and also to send them the Christmas brochure produced by the charity's trading company.

The new donor hasn't had a chance to opt out of future marketing, and Barbara realises that they might intend their donation as a one-off. She deals with this in her thank-you letter. She includes a paragraph saying: 'We expect you would like to hear from us about how we are using your donation and how you can continue to support us in future. However, if you would prefer us not to contact you, please let me know (contact details above). Similarly, we would like to send you a Christmas catalogue, but do let me know if you would prefer not to receive it.'

Across town, Brian takes a different line. In the same situation he assumes that someone who is keen enough to send an unsolicited donation won't mind getting occasional mailings. He adds the donor to his database without mentioning anything in the thank-you letter. Of course if they subsequently object he will mark their record to receive no further mailings, but he gets very few complaints so feels that his approach is reasonable. (Brian and Barbara often argue amicably about this when they meet up.)

Sylvia inherits an old database when she takes up a new fundraising post. She has no idea what information people were given when their details were originally collected. Although the data is quite old, it seems likely that most of it is still fairly accurate and that the people are good prospects. Sylvia decides that it would be reasonable to send them an appeal. She does this after checking the names against the organisation's suppression list (in case any of them have already said they don't want to receive fundraising mailings). She makes it clear in her letter that she knows it is a while since the organisation was in touch with these people, and tells them how to contact her if they definitely don't want to hear from the organisation again.

Chapter 13

Subject Access

The Data Subject's right to see the information you hold on them is a significant safeguard against information being used wrongly or held inaccurately. It is important to get Subject Access right, because people who make a request are often already at odds with the Data Controller, and any mistakes will only make a bad situation worse.

This chapter looks at:

- The process involved in giving Data Subjects access to information
- The information the Data Subject has the right to see
- The relatively limited exemptions from access

In principle a Data Subject has the right to know *all* the Personal Data that you hold about them. This is known as the right of Subject Access.

This right has not been much used. Most large voluntary organisations will have had experience of handling a few Subject Access requests, but many smaller organisations are unlikely to have received any at all. Nevertheless it is an important right, and if you are a Data Controller you need to be fully aware of it. The fact that under the 1998 Act it applies to much manual data as well as computer records adds complications to the handling of Subject Access requests.

The basic position is that when someone makes a valid Subject Access request you have to:

- tell them whether any of their Personal Data is being processed by you, or for you by a Data Processor;
- give them a description of the data, why you hold it and who it may be disclosed to;
- supply a copy of all the Personal Data you hold about that Data Subject;
- say where you got the information from, if you know;

- explain the logic involved in any automated decision you make about that Data Subject, unless it is a trade secret.

There are qualifications to some of these provisions, discussed later in the chapter.

Some organisations feel that it can be beneficial to allow the Data Subject to inspect their records if they wish, rather than providing them with a copy (although if they then want a copy of all or part of the record you still have to provide it). This has the advantage that any questions the Data Subject has may be answered straight away, and support can be offered if the content of the records may be upsetting. If you adopt this policy, it is important to ensure that the access is supervised, to prevent any possibility of tampering, and that the file is checked first to ensure that information which the Data Subject is not entitled to see has been temporarily removed.

In all cases it may also be worth asking the Data Subject if they want access to their whole record, or if they are only interested in a particular type of material, issue or time period. This can help to reduce your workload, and also give them a quicker and more useful response. However, the choice is theirs; if they want a copy of everything, subject to the exclusions discussed later in the chapter, they can have it.

What is a valid Subject Access request?

A Subject Access request must be made in writing; it may be sent by electronic means such as fax or e-mail.

You may, but do not have to, charge a fee of up to £10. There is nothing to stop you having a different fee for different circumstances, or different types of Data Subject. If you ask the Data Subject for a fee and they do not pay, you do not have to respond to the Subject Access request.

You must be careful to provide the information only to the right person. This means that you may, and probably should, ask for information to verify their identity.

If the request is made on behalf of the Data Subject by a third party, such as a solicitor or a parent, you must check not just the Data Subject's identity, but also that the person making the request is properly authorised to do so (see Chapter 4). In most cases it would be wise to get written evidence of authorisation.

> **We've had a Subject Access request from the absent parent of a child whose data we hold. Do we have to comply?**
>
> First, you should check that the child is not old enough to exercise their own Data Protection rights. These could override any wishes of the parents (see Chapter 4). Then you need to be confident that the parent has a legal right to act on behalf of the child. If all is in order, you do have to comply.

You may also ask for information to help you locate the Data Subject's records. You might, for example, want to ask if they had ever been a client, or a volunteer, or which branch of your organisation they originally dealt with. You can only ask for 'reasonable' information, and even if the Data Subject can't answer your questions, you still have to make a reasonable attempt to find any data you have on them.

Once you have received a valid Subject Access request you must reply 'promptly' and within a maximum of 40 calendar (not working) days.

You may choose to respond to an invalid Subject Access request (for example, one made verbally) if you wish, but you might run the risk of overlooking an important step. It is probably better to insist on a written application in most cases.

You do not have to respond if a Subject Access request is made too soon after an identical or similar request from the same Data Subject. In deciding whether it is too soon, you have to consider the type of data, your purpose(s) in holding it and how often it changes.

A Subject Access request form

You cannot insist on people using a specific form for making a Subject Access request, but you may feel that having one would help your Data Subjects. If you do, you could consider including sections that ask for:

- the date, so that you can calculate the 40-day response limit;
- the name of the Data Subject (and any previous names);
- an address to which the reply should be sent;
- any information that you need to verify the Data Subject's identity;
- any information that you need to help you find the records;
- your fee;
- a signature;
- evidence of authorisation if the person applying is not the Data Subject.

It may be worth describing on the form the process that you will follow, and stating the time limit or any self-imposed targets for response. You may also want to give general information, for example about the purposes for which you process Personal Data. A sample form is given on page 88.

What information do you have to provide?

In responding to a Subject Access request, you must in principle provide all the Personal Data you hold about the Data Subject. You must provide a copy of the information in 'permanent form', unless:

Data Protection

- it is not possible; or
- it would involve disproportionate effort; or
- the Data Subject has agreed otherwise.

The information must be 'intelligible' to the Data Subject. This means that you must, for example, explain any codes used.

You must provide the information that you held at the time when the Subject Access request was made, except that you are allowed to make routine changes. For example, if you sell publications and a customer asks for a copy of their record and, in the meantime, you receive a payment from them, you are allowed to update their record. You can even delete the information altogether *if you would have done it anyway*. For example, you might take people's details in order to send them a brochure, then delete the information once the brochure has been sent. Someone might make a Subject Access request only to find that by the time you responded you legitimately no longer held any information about them.

What you certainly *must not do* is tamper with the information to remove parts you would rather the Data Subject didn't see, or do anything to it that you wouldn't have done in the normal course of events.

A Subject Access request applies to *all* the Personal Data held by the Data Controller to whom the request is made. If your records are scattered around – in various databases, and in different files held by different people – your task will be that much harder when it comes to finding and collating it all in order to respond. Good information management and good Data Protection practice coincide: get your information organised properly and it will be much easier to comply with Subject Access requests and other Data Protection requirements.

Do we have to show people references when they make a Subject Access request?

You don't have to show them any confidential references you have given. You may have to show references you have received, unless the referee has withheld consent and is being reasonable. See also Appendix C.

Note that you have to provide a copy of the *information* you hold, not a copy of the *documents* on which the information is held. It is acceptable, therefore, to print out an extract from a database record, or from a longer document, or even to retype a hand-written document, provided the information is still accurately represented. This may be particularly relevant if you are 'redacting' a document – removing or hiding parts of the information which the Data Subject is not entitled to see (see page 90).

Sample Subject Access request form

Date received:_____

NAME OF ORGANISATION

Subject Access request (1998 Data Protection Act)

You are entitled to see most of the information we hold about you. If you want to see it, please fill in this form and hand it in to the office, with the £10 fee.

Your name: _____

Your address: _____

A phone number where we can contact you (if you wish): _____

Please tick if you have ever been:

[ ] an employee   [ ] a client at our main office

[ ] a volunteer in our office   [ ] a client at our branch office

If you have not ticked any of the above, please tell us of any reason why you think we might have information about you: _____

_____

If we may have known you under a different name, please tell us here:

_____

If you are only interested in particular information, please say what that is:

_____

I want to see the records you hold on me, and I enclose £10. Signature: _____

Please note:

- If the address you give above does not match the one in our records, we may have to ask you for additional identification.
- If you are not the Data Subject (the person the information is about), we will need evidence that you are authorised to act for the Subject.
- We will reply as quickly as we can. We aim to reply within three weeks, but we may take up to 40 days. If you have asked for a copy of the information, we will send it to the address you have given above.
- We have information about members of our organisation, staff, volunteers, clients and people we think might be interested in our work. We don't keep this information once we no longer need it, so if you were in touch with us some time ago we may no longer have any information about you.
- We will provide everything we have about you, except that we may be allowed to hold back information which is also about, or which identifies, someone else.

Information you do not have to provide

Although in principle you have to provide the Data Subject with a copy of everything, there are exceptions, including the following examples.

- You may be able to hold back 'third party' material (see below).
- You do not have to provide any confidential reference you have *sent* (but you may have to show those you have *received*).
- You do not have to provide information used for 'management forecasting or management planning' if this would 'prejudice the conduct' of your business.
- You can hold back details of your intentions in any negotiations if this would ruin your bargaining position.
- Material subject to legal professional privilege (or the equivalent in Scotland) can be held back.
- There are various exemptions relating to examination marks and scripts.

'Third party' information is any information that identifies an individual other than the Data Subject. Material qualifies as third party information:

- if the other person can be identified as the source of the information; *or*
- if information about them is included in it – as a family member, a witness to an incident, even just in the background of a photograph, for example; *and*
- if you have any reason to believe that the Data Subject could identify the other person. For example, in a dispute between neighbours, even an anonymous complaint might come from someone whom the Data Subject can easily identify.

However, 'third party' material is not automatically excluded. You do have to provide the information about the other person if:

- that person has given their consent; or
- it is reasonable to go ahead without their consent.

In deciding whether it is reasonable to go ahead without consent, you have to take account of:

- any duty of confidentiality you owe to the other person;
- anything you have done to try to get their consent;
- whether they are able to give consent;
- whether they have refused consent;
- harm that may be caused to the Data Subject by not disclosing the information, set against the harm that may be done to the third party by disclosing it.

> **Can a manager refuse access to their comments on staff because of the third party rule?**
>
> No. It is very unlikely. There is no special exemption from Subject Access for opinions about the Data Subject. Although the manager may be a third party, they are acting as an agent of the Data Controller. It is hard to see how a refusal of consent could be 'reasonable' unless they have given the comments in confidence and can claim that a duty of confidentiality applies.

If you have consent, or if it is reasonable to go ahead without consent, then you *must* include the information about the other person in your response to the Subject Access request. You can also choose to include the information even if you don't have to, but you would have to be careful. For example, if the other person was also a Data Subject of yours, you would have to be sure that revealing the information when you didn't have to was 'fair'. You may also owe the third party a duty of confidentiality.

If you are certain that the information is something the Data Subject already knows – such as the names of family members living in their house – you may be quite happy to release it without seeking consent. In other cases you may want to check first whether you have any information about them that they would rather the Data Subject didn't see.

> **Social services provides us with a lot of information about clients that is marked 'confidential'. Is it OK to withhold this when a client makes a Subject Access request?**
>
> There is no automatic right to withhold information just because it is marked 'confidential'. While social services departments do have powers to withhold information in certain cases, these powers do not extend to information provided by social services to another Data Controller. If they really want to restrict access, they should think twice about giving you the information or come up with a convincing argument for you having a duty of confidentiality that would override Data Protection requirements.

Where you regularly obtain information from other people, or where your records are likely to contain information about more than just the Data Subject, you may need to think ahead about whether you want to withhold it.

One option is to have an 'open files' policy. If people who give you information know in advance that it will automatically be shown to the Data Subject in response to a request, and that they will be identified, you would have good grounds for arguing that it was reasonable to give the information without going back to seek consent. This might be appropriate where the information comes from people who are providing it professionally (such as managers in a personnel system, or care workers in a client records system). They would have little reason to insist on anonymity.

In other cases you may want to assure people that the information they give will be held confidentially. Then you would have good grounds for withholding it from Subject Access, but you still have to try to obtain consent.

Subject Access to e-mails

E-mails are unlikely to constitute Personal Data about the staff member who sent them just by virtue of including their e-mail address and name. However, they may contain Personal Data – either about the staff member or about someone else. This would mean that you may be required to produce the e-mails in response to a Subject Access request.

The Information Commissioner appears to have withdrawn a previous guidance note on Subject Access to e-mails. The gist of this was that a general trawl of the whole computer system to find e-mails relating to the individual would probably not be required, but that a detailed search might be necessary if the Data Subject had given sufficient help to find them – such as who they were sent to or by, and when.

This position is unlikely to have changed significantly. You should in any case be prepared to search your live e-mail system, and your archives for any period where you have reason to believe relevant e-mails might be held.

Social work, medical and education exemptions

Parts of social work, medical and education records may be withheld from Subject Access in certain cases, which are set out in supplementary Regulations.[32] The Act and Regulations define in detail which records are covered. Normally, records held by voluntary organisations are unlikely to be included. For example the social work exemptions apply to a voluntary organisation only if:

- the organisation has been 'designated' by the Secretary of State for Health; *and*
- it is essentially carrying out local authority social work functions.

At the time of writing, the only voluntary organisation 'designated' was the NSPCC, and there has been no indication that the government is keen to extend the list.

The general ground for withholding information under all these Regulations is that disclosure would 'cause serious harm to the physical or mental health or condition of the Data Subject or another person'. In the case of medical records this has to be assessed by an appropriate medical practitioner. An employer could not, for example, decide to withhold the results of medical tests carried out on their behalf.

---

32 Statutory Instruments 2000 Nos. 413, 414 and 415.

Subject access to third party material

NB: This is only to do with Subject Access; it doesn't affect disclosure to others.

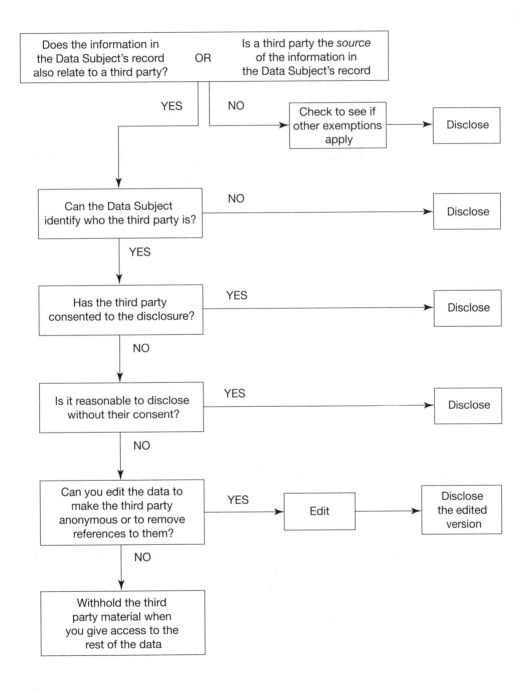

Practical steps

Although you may never have to deal with a Subject Access request, you do need to be prepared. Among other things, you should consider the following steps.

- All your staff and volunteers, particularly those who deal with clients or the public, must be made aware that a Subject Access request has a legal status and that they must promptly pass it on to the appropriate person in the organisation.

- You may want to draw up a Subject Access request form (see page 88).

- You should ensure when you design information systems that you make it as easy as possible to locate all the information about any particular Data Subject. (See also Appendix E.)

- You have to tell the Data Subject, when you respond, what sort of disclosures you make and any information you have about the sources of your information. Because of this, you may want to design systems to record your sources and disclosures.

- You may want to consider your policy on withholding information about other people (see previous page).

- Your trustees or management committee will need to decide your policy on charging for Subject Access.

Above all, because mistakes with Subject Access can have serious consequences, you should consider taking qualified legal advice if you are in any doubt about whether you should respond to the request or show specific pieces of information.

Further guidance on several aspects of Subject Access is available on the Information Commissioner's website.

Summary

- Individuals have a right to see most of the data you hold about them.

- You have to reply promptly to a Subject Access request, and within 40 days at most.

- You may charge up to £10 to reply to a Subject Access request.

- You must generally provide, in permanent form, a copy of all the data about the Subject that you held at the time when the Subject Access request was made.

- In certain cases you are allowed to withhold access to information that identifies other people.

Examples

1) Lee is responsible for personnel administration in a medium-sized charity. One of the workers asks to see her file, but Lee is worried because the file contains an old note from her previous line manager that is not wholly complimentary. Suppressing the urge just to 'lose' the note, Lee has to decide whether there are any grounds for withholding it. He eventually concludes that he should not hold it back, since it was not given in confidence, and the line manager wrote it in the course of his work. For the future Lee resolves that personnel files should not contain this type of material.

2) A mediation service does not always manage to win the trust of potential clients. Some of them start to make Subject Access requests in order to 'see what people are saying about me'. Linda, the manager, decides on a twofold strategy. First, most of the records will be kept in paper files. Clients who have agreed to work with the service each get their own file, but until then the information is not readily accessible, and therefore not Personal Data. Second, the service will extend its policy on confidentiality, to make it clear that information provided by or related to other people will never be disclosed without their consent.

Chapter 14

Security

Security is clearly one of the most important Data Protection issues. Unauthorised access to information is a big risk, and the harm that could result from information getting into the wrong hands is considerable. This requires not just written policies, but staff who understand fully how to maintain high levels of confidentiality in their day-to-day work.

This chapter looks at:

- The requirements of the Act
- Some possible measures to consider

Security is about making sure that the data you hold is available to you when you need it, and to no one else.

> **The seventh Data Protection Principle**
>
> Appropriate technical and organisational measures shall be taken against unauthorised or unlawful processing of Personal Data and against accidental loss or destruction of, or damage to, Personal Data.

There are two types of security breach you have to protect against:

- processing that is not authorised by you or is unlawful;
- data getting damaged, lost or destroyed.

The measures you take must be both technical (locks, passwords, back-ups and so on) and organisational (including procedures, training, supervision and management systems).

When a Data Controller has to make a notification (see Chapter 21), this must include a statement about the security measures in place. The Information Commissioner has said that if a Data Controller has implemented BS7799[33] (the British Standard for Information Security Management) this will represent the type of assurance that the Commissioner is looking for. The questions asked on the notification application form reflect the approach taken by BS7799, and you are prompted to confirm that you broadly follow that approach.

BS7799 itself is complex and expensive to implement, and is unlikely to be worth pursuing for most voluntary organisations. This does not mean that security can be ignored, however.

What is 'appropriate'?

Your security must be appropriate. The security measures you need to take will depend very much on the risk that would result from the data being unavailable or getting into the wrong hands in any way. Your approach should be similar to that in a risk assessment.

- How many people could be harmed by any specific risk?
- How likely is it to happen?
- How great would the damage be if it did?

Information that you could easily replace would obviously not merit such great security as that which would take considerable time and effort to replace, or which may be completely irreplaceable. Highly confidential information would need more protection than that which is already in the public domain.

Some of your security measures will be general, and aimed at protecting you against disruption as much as anything. Making back-ups and checking incoming electronic material for viruses should be part of everyone's routine procedures. So should making sure that you know who is in the building, and that strangers are not allowed to wander around unsupervised.

We need highly sensitive health information about the children we take out on trips. What is appropriate security for this? We can't lock it away because then it wouldn't necessarily be available quickly in an emergency.

Obviously you need to take some precautions. However, all you may need is something as simple as a folder, kept in an unobtrusive place, which you mark clearly with the words 'Confidential: For use by the team leader or their authorised deputy only'. Provided all the other adult leaders on the trip understand that 'confidential' means confidential, this may be sufficient. Other information that has to be generally available must, of course, be kept in a different folder, and possibly in a different place.

---

33 Also known as ISO 17799.

You should also take those specific additional measures which protect most effectively against the most serious risks. With confidential client files, for example, you may want to have a procedure for signing them in and out of a secure area, to allow for times when your staff may need to take material out to meetings or case conferences. If you regularly deliver some of your services off the premises – at outreach sessions or in people's homes, for example – this might be a particular concern.

If staff or volunteers work from home at all you will need to think about how to ensure that your security measures extend to their laptops (which may get stolen), their home computers (which may be used by other family members) or their kitchen tables, which are all intrinsically insecure areas.

Do I have to buy lockable filing cabinets for all my staff who work from home?

It might be worth considering, but the main thing is to make sure that they know their responsibilities. A lockable cabinet wouldn't help if someone is in the habit of leaving confidential case files on the kitchen table while the neighbours drop in for tea. Provided the person has somewhere suitable to work, which allows them to store papers out of the way of casual visitors, you may decide to put most of your effort into training on confidentiality and security. You should do a risk assessment to help you set your priorities.

Unauthorised access

From the fact that you have to prevent unauthorised access, it follows that you have to be clear what kinds of access are authorised. This should cover the following points.

- Internal access – who on your staff is allowed access to the information, and for what purpose(s)? This is usually best set out in your confidentiality policy (see Chapter 17).
- External access – who outside your organisation is allowed access, and under what circumstances? For example, how do they have to prove their identity, and what methods of disclosing information do you consider secure?

Far more security breaches come about through inadvertent, mischievous or deliberate misuse of data by people who are entitled to have it, than by external intrusion. This could mean people looking at files that they know (or should know) they are not allowed to see, or leaving information around where other people can easily read it. Equally, you should think about how you might prevent staff from giving information over the telephone that should not be given out in this way unless you are sure you are giving it to the right person.

The rules should apply equally to permanent staff, volunteers, temporary and sessional staff, management committee members, consultants and any other people who act on your behalf. It is not enough to assume that all these people understand what is meant by confidentiality and security. Your regular receptionist may be quite clear that staff members' home numbers are not given out; this week's temp may not. Security and confidentiality should be a standard part of the induction for anyone new to your organisation, and should be a regular part of staff briefings, to keep it in the forefront of everyone's mind.

Our management committee feels that they should be able to look at any files they choose to, including confidential client case records. Is this right?

No. They can only look at papers they are authorised to see. And the organisation should be careful, when it authorises access, to respect the second Data Protection Principle which says that all processing must be compatible with the purpose(s) data is held for. If you are offering a confidential service, it is unlikely to be 'compatible' for people to look at the data if there is no operational need for them to do so.

Access control

To prevent people gaining unauthorised access to information, even without meaning to, you may need to consider any or all of the following questions.

- Do your staff members and volunteers know which information they are allowed to see and which not?

- Do your staff and volunteers (including temporary staff and consultants) sign an unambiguous confidentiality statement? (See Chapter 17.)

- Do you require external contractors (such as computer maintenance staff) to give confidentiality undertakings?

- Have your staff and volunteers been trained or briefed on how to keep data secure?

- Are your confidential files in a protected area and/or locked away when not in use?

- Are you careful not to allow unauthorised people to be left on their own in the presence of Personal Data?

- Do you clear your working area of Personal Data before leaving the office?

- Are your computers sited so that people cannot see material on the screen that they shouldn't?

- Does your computer system prevent people from leaving Personal Data on the screen for too long (for example when they leave their desk, or when the next client has already arrived)?

- Do you encrypt or password-protect Personal Data, especially when you send it by e-mail?

- Is your website isolated from your internal systems and protected from hackers?

- Do you have a system to keep track of Personal Data that people take out of the office?

- If people are allowed to see some material, but not all of it, do your systems help to enforce this, by storing the information in different places or by requiring a different password for the more sensitive material?

- Do you force people to change passwords and access codes often enough (especially when staff leave)?

- When you deliberately delete material from your computer, do you have the facility to overwrite it to make sure that it is irrecoverable?

- Are confidential manual files shredded or securely disposed of?

Protecting data while it is in transit

Many of the most high profile breaches of Data Protection security involve the loss of data in transit, or when it is away from the office. One of the most dramatic was the loss in 2007 by HM Revenue & Customs of the personal details of 25 million people when information relating to Child Benefit was sent by courier to the National Audit Office. In that case, the data was not sent by secure means, and it was also not encrypted, so that it would have been easily accessible to anyone who had found it or intercepted it.

Other cases – both from government and commercial organisations – have involved the loss of laptop computers or portable media, such as USB sticks, containing significant amounts of Personal Data, and the sale of redundant computers and components, without the data having been securely wiped from them.

While perfect security is neither possible nor expected, you should take careful steps to provide an appropriate level of protection. This means, for example:

- not taking more information out of the office than you need. Don't take a large file containing the details of many people; extract the information you need to work on and take just that;

- guarding the information carefully when you take it out – having suitable means of transporting equipment, so that it is less likely to be left lying around or stolen, locking it in the boot of the car instead of leaving it on the seat, and so on. It is worth remembering that very small devices – even a mobile phone – can nowadays contain a significant amount of Personal Data;

- thinking about how you transmit information. E-mail is often more secure than putting a disk in the post, and it is worth investigating the options for protecting disks and individual files by passwords and encryption if they contain significant amounts of Personal Data.

At the time of writing the Information Commissioner was suggesting that substantial negligence by individuals leading to loss of data should be made a criminal offence, instead of the whole responsibility lying with the Data Controller – who would only be liable for any actual harm caused by the breach, not for the distress or inconvenience such a loss could cause.

Unauthorised access as a criminal offence

Individuals who breach security are committing a criminal offence if they do so 'knowingly or recklessly', or allow other people access to data without authorisation. It is also an offence to sell data obtained without authorisation.

The offence is committed when an individual goes against instructions. It is one of the few breaches of the Act that are specifically an individual, rather than a corporate, responsibility. This offence can be defended on the grounds that the person had the 'reasonable belief' that the action was permissible. This is yet another argument for having a clear policy on confidentiality and an organisational culture that respects it.

There have been numerous prosecutions for this offence, ranging from blatant attempts to con information out of people, to situations which the perpetrator probably thought were innocuous. The following are just a few examples.

- In April 2004, a company director was fined almost £3,000 because his employees, involved in debt collection, sought information under false pretences over the telephone.

- In October 2005, a private detective was fined £6,250 plus £600 costs for unlawfully obtaining information from medical centres, as well as misrepresenting himself to HM Revenue & Customs.

- In 2006, a couple working for a private detective had to pay £14,800 in fines and costs for 'blagging' information about their targets' bank account details, income tax information and ex-directory phone numbers from organisations including HM Revenue & Customs and BT.

- In July 2004, a 'bored' computer operator working for Gwent Police was fined £400 for using control room computers to investigate people she knew.

- In January 2005, a special constable in Dorset was fined £1,000 with £500 costs for using a police database to investigate colleagues she suspected of stealing from her workplace.

In the first three examples, the people involved must have known they were doing wrong. The remaining two, however, were instances where the person legitimately had access to the computer system, but were not authorised to do so for that purpose. In those cases, the actual potential harm was probably negligible – as indicated by the size of the penalties – but the principle was important enough to bring the case.

Typically, fines have been around £300 per offence, but in many cases there have been multiple offences, leading to fines of thousands of pounds, plus costs.

While your staff and volunteers are, presumably, unlikely to access information deliberately without authorisation, you may find it worth pointing out the legal position to them. It is not unknown, for example, for a disgruntled volunteer to walk off with an organisation's membership list and try to set up a rival organisation, or for a staff member to break into the confidential personnel filing cabinet to find out what the organisation's lawyers were advising in a disciplinary case. Both of these actions could potentially land the individual in court.

Database copyright

In addition to Data Protection restrictions on access, you should also be aware of the copyright protection for databases (whether these contain information about individual people or not).[34]

A case in 2008 found against two ex-employees who took details from a firm's customer database on their departure. The question of whether the information was confidential was immaterial; merely taking the information was a breach of copyright. While the criminal offence of unauthorised access is in some ways more serious, breach of copyright is a civil matter, which means that an organisation could take action for an injunction and/or damages directly, without having to involve the police in a prosecution.

Another aspect of database copyright is that copyright usually resides with the creator of the material in question. If you outsource work and your contract with the Data Processor is not correctly drafted, then the Data Processor may end up owning the rights in any information they collect. Any contract with a Data Processor should therefore include an assignment of the intellectual property in any database (or any other 'creative' work) that the Data Processor produces, develops or uses on your behalf.

Loss or damage

Data in electronic form is particularly vulnerable to loss or damage as a result of computer failure and other technical problems. Manual data must not be overlooked, however. You may need to consider the following questions.

- Are your staff and volunteers aware of all the precautions they need to take? Have they been trained in back-up and other procedures?

---

34 Implementation of European Directive 96/9/EC under the Copyright and Rights in Databases Regulations 1997, which amended the Copyright, Designs And Patents Act 1988.

- Are irreplaceable documents protected from fire (especially if you ever hold original documents on behalf of service users)?

- Do you avoid taking irreplaceable documents out of the building whenever possible?

- Are your computer systems backed up rigorously and frequently enough, using a recognised procedure? Are back-ups stored off site?

- Do you test your back-ups to ensure they can be restored?

- Do your computer users know how to set their software to make automatic back-ups?

- Do you protect your organisation against computer viruses?

- Do your systems require confirmation before significant material can be deleted?

- Do you give meaningful and consistent names to your files, so that they are less likely to be deleted inadvertently?

- Have you taken adequate precautions to avoid key computers being stolen?

- Do your staff and volunteers take steps to protect computers against damage, especially from liquids or physical damage?

- Do you have a disaster recovery plan?

Encryption

Although the Data Protection Act does not mandate particular security measures, saying merely that security measures must be 'appropriate', the consensus on what this means may change over time. In response to a case in 2007,[35] for example, the Information Commissioner required the Department of Health in future to encrypt any Personal Data on its website which could cause distress to individuals if disclosed.

Encryption – or usually the lack of it – has also been a feature of many other cases where data was lost in transit, stolen, mislaid or unintentionally sold on redundant equipment.

Although encryption is not a complete security solution, and certainly not enough on its own, it does now appear that it must be considered seriously for data which is likely to leave your organisation, or which is particularly confidential.

British Standard 7799

If you are reviewing your security, it may be worth considering the approach taken in the British Standard, BS7799. This identifies ten key controls for information security.

---

35 A security breach on the Medical Training Application Service website.

- Is there a documented security policy?
- Are responsibilities for security processes clearly allocated?
- Are users given adequate security training?
- Are security incidents always reported?
- Is there a virus-checking policy?
- Is there a plan for maintaining business continuity?
- Are legal copyright issues always given due consideration?
- Are important organisational records protected?
- Are personal records processed in accordance with the Data Protection Act?
- Are regular security reviews performed?

These controls provide for the basic level of information security. However, BS7799 also covers measures necessary to achieve a higher level of security, including:

- more on policies and management of security;
- asset classification and control;
- personnel security;
- physical and environmental security;
- computer and network management;
- system access control;
- systems development and maintenance;
- business continuity planning;
- compliance with all relevant laws.

Implementing BS7799 itself is carried out on a commercial basis by the British Standards Institution and other bodies. It involves assessment, advice and audit procedures, and leads to certification which lasts for three years.

Summary

- You must have security measures that are appropriate to the type of Personal Data you hold and to how it is used. These must prevent unauthorised access as well as inadvertent loss or damage.
- You must describe your security measures when you notify your processing to the Information Commissioner.
- BS7799 covers information security management, but is complex and expensive to implement.

Examples

1) Malcolm runs a dial-a-ride service. One day, one of the drivers leaves his pick-up list on top of the minibus by mistake and drives off. The details of his clients, including when they will be away from home and information about their disabilities, go floating off for anyone to find.

   Malcolm realises that this is a potentially serious security breach. He modifies the minibus dashboard so that there is a recognised place to secure the pick-up lists. He changes procedures so that the lists have to be signed in and out, and briefs all the staff on why he has done this. He reports to the committee, which is satisfied that he has taken 'appropriate' technical and organisational measures both to improve security and to ensure that any future problem is identified as early as possible.

2) Most of the volunteers at Sarah's drop-in centre for older people come from the local community. One day she overhears two of them exchanging gossip about several of the centre users, which they have picked up in the course of their work. Some of the information is 'sensitive'. Sarah quickly stops them, and realises that many of the volunteers are likely to know users of the centre, or have them as neighbours. In this situation it is particularly important to be responsible about the use of information they acquire about users. Sarah organises a training session on confidentiality for all the volunteers, and strengthens the centre's policy so that volunteers have to sign a statement clearly agreeing not to discuss with each other any information that is in the client files.

3) Martha works at a large residential home. A new computer system is introduced for holding residents' details, which includes a lot of 'sensitive' information. The centre manager and shift leaders are trained in how to use it, and given passwords which allow access to all the information, while other workers are allowed to access only basic parts of the record.

   One day Martha needs to look up the phone number of a resident's daughter to discuss a change of room with her. When she goes to the computer she finds that the centre manager has been using it, and has been called away urgently, leaving the database open on a very sensitive screen which Martha is normally not able to see. Martha hasn't been told what to do in this situation, or how to close the screen and get back to her normal view of the data. She mentions the incident to her shift leader.

   The shift leader's first response is to blame Martha for getting unauthorised access to the data, but Martha manages to convince him that it wasn't her fault. Instead, they compile a report to the information steering group. The group concludes that:

   - the centre manager should not have left the screen open; however, since she was called away in a genuine emergency they decide to take no further action;

- it would be better if the system was redesigned to shut down sensitive screens automatically after a set interval of no activity;
- all staff should be given extra training in what to do if they find the system behaving differently from usual.

Chapter 15

Transferring Personal Data abroad

Having taken the trouble to protect data in this country, you should try to ensure that it stays protected if it goes abroad. Relatively few voluntary organisations transfer information directly to other organisations abroad. Many are likely, however, to include Personal Data in information they publish on their website. In both these instances the organisations are potentially transferring Personal Data abroad under the terms of the Data Protection Act.

This chapter explains:

- The restrictions that apply to transferring Personal Data abroad
- The options available to organisations wanting to transfer Personal Data

The eighth Data Protection Principle imposes restrictions on the transfer of Personal Data to countries where it is not protected by law. The aim of the Principle is to ensure that Data Subjects do not lose any of their rights when their Personal Data is transferred abroad. The Principle is modified by Schedule 4 of the Act.

The eighth Data Protection Principle

Personal Data shall not be transferred to a country or territory outside the European Economic Area unless that country or territory ensures an adequate level of protection for the rights and freedoms of data subjects in relation to the processing of Personal Data.

It is important to realise that putting data on a website could constitute an overseas transfer. For more on this, see Chapter 18.

Transferring Personal Data without further restrictions

For some countries there are no restrictions other than those which would apply to the use of data within the UK. These countries are:

- the countries of the European Economic Area (EEA);
- those additional countries that have been accepted by the European Commission as having adequate Data Protection legislation.

The EEA comprises the European Union (at the time of writing this includes Austria, Belgium, Bulgaria, Cyprus, Czech Republic, Denmark, Estonia, Finland, France, Germany, Greece, Hungary, Ireland, Italy, Latvia, Lithuania, Luxembourg, Malta, the Netherlands, Poland, Portugal, Romania, Slovakia, Slovenia, Spain, Sweden and the United Kingdom) plus Iceland, Liechtenstein and Norway.[36]

From time to time the European Commission announces its decisions on whether other countries, outside the EEA, have adequate legal protection. At the time of writing, decisions have been made that Argentina, Canada, Guernsey, the Isle of Man and Switzerland provide adequate legal protection. (Jersey has a law, but for some reason no decision has been made.)

The situation regarding the USA is complex. The USA has no general Data Protection law but, after prolonged and at times acrimonious negotiation, the European Commission agreed that the 'Safe Harbor' scheme provides an adequate level of protection in the USA.

When a US company signs up to the Safe Harbor arrangement, it agrees to follow seven principles of information handling. It also agrees that it can be held responsible for keeping to those principles by the Federal Trade Commission. The scheme is not well used. At the time of writing, fewer than 1,500 companies were listed as having signed up.[37]

In addition, the EU and the USA have negotiated a succession of agreements, the most recent in July 2007, on the transfer of passenger name record information from EU airlines to the US Department of Homeland Security (DHS).

This unsatisfactory situation is largely the result of not only unwillingness in the USA to take seriously European concerns about the privacy and security of Personal Data, but also anxiety in Europe about the economic and political effects of restricting the transfer of data. The result nevertheless is that, for most purposes, the USA has to be treated as a country where adequate Data Protection is not available under law.

---

36 Note, however, that the Channel Islands and the Isle of Man are not in the EEA.
37 See www.export.gov/safeharbor

Transferring Personal Data when restrictions apply

With few exceptions, you must not transfer Personal Data outside the countries previously discussed, unless the protection it will receive is 'adequate'.

A paper on the Information Commissioner's website discusses overseas transfers – and in particular adequacy – in some detail.[38] The Commissioner argues that it is better to provide adequate protection for Personal Data than to use exemptions under which the transfer is permitted even though protection may be lost.

Where you transfer information to countries that are not in the EEA and which have not been approved, it is open to you as a Data Controller to make your own decision on adequacy – or even to decide that the information being transferred is so trivial that it is 'adequate' to have no protection at all. In making this decision, most will prefer to follow the Commissioner's guidance.

When your overseas transfer is to a fixed set of organisations, and especially if you can identify significant risks to your Data Subjects, you should first consider whether it is possible to make contractual arrangements[39] with the recipient organisation(s) overseas under which the Data Subject's rights are protected. Standard terms have been approved by the European Commission, details of which can be obtained from the Information Commissioner's website. (The original set of standard terms were not popular with business, being described as 'neither user-friendly nor commercially sensible'.[40] Revised rules issued in 2005 have been much better received.)

Where the transfer is within your organisation – for example to a branch or subsidiary overseas – the equivalent to a contract is 'binding corporate rules'.

We send details of supporters to our partner organisations in India, so that they can send information about their work directly to the supporters. Should we ask for their consent?

You should first consider whether it would be possible to have a contract with your partner organisations which protects the Personal Data. If this is not possible you would only be able to transfer the data with consent from your Data Subjects. In either case, they should be fully informed before their data is transferred.

---

38 International transfers of personal information: general advice on how to comply with the 8th data protection principle.

39 In the past there used to be a problem in deriving terms for the transfer of Personal Data that the Commissioner could approve. This difficulty was removed when the law in England and Wales was amended by the Contracts (Rights of Third Parties) Act 1999 to permit a contract between two parties to grant rights to a third party. Scotland already had such a provision.

40 In 2005 by Shelagh Gaskill, a partner at Pinsent Masons.

> **We recruit volunteers to work with organisations overseas. Do we need consent before we can send their details to the organisation they will be working for?**
>
> Again, you should look at contracts with the host organisations in the first place. Only if you decide that this is impractical, or that the risk is acceptable, could you ask for consent. Be aware, however, of the Information Commissioner's view that consent is 'unlikely to be valid if the individual has no choice but to give their consent'.

Although protecting Personal Data properly will be the appropriate course of action in most cases, there are exemptions available. The two exemptions most likely to apply to voluntary organisations are:

- to have the consent of the Data Subject;
- for the processing to be *necessary* in connection with a contract involving the Data Subject, or a contract that is in their interests.

Although these are discouraged, they may very well be appropriate in one-off and low-risk situations.

If you seek consent for transfers abroad, this should be approached in the same way as consent under Schedule 2 (see Chapter 8). It is not safe to assume that Data Subjects will understand the full implications of a transfer abroad. To have 'informed' consent, therefore, it would be wise to explain that data transferred abroad will not be protected to the same extent as it is in the UK.

> **We send staff to work outside Europe. Do we need consent before we can send details of the staff concerned to the organisations they will be working alongside?**
>
> Probably not. If the transfer of data is *necessary* for a contract which the Data Subject is party to, or which is in their interests, you do not need consent. However, if you cannot guarantee the protection of the information, you should ensure that your staff are aware of this.

The exemption for information concerning a contract applies only if the transfer is necessary. A clear example of this is travel. If you were sending your staff to a conference in Russia, for example, it would be necessary to provide their details to the conference organiser, the hotel, the airline and so on. Whether the contract for these services is with the Data Subject or the Data Controller doesn't matter, provided the contract is in the Data Subject's interests. You must, however, limit the information to what is necessary and, in order to be fair, you may want to remind the Data Subjects that they will not have the same control over the use of any data transferred in this way.

We send people abroad to raise funds for us on a challenge which is organised by an external company. What are the Data Protection implications?

First you need to establish whether the Data Controller is your organisation, with the challenge organiser acting as Data Processor, or whether the challenge organiser is a Data Controller in their own right. This will probably depend on how involved you are in the organising. Whoever is the Data Controller then needs to assess whether the arrangements are subject to one or more contracts (not necessarily ones the Data Subject is party to). If contracts cannot be put in place, any necessary transfers need consent.

Summary

Transferring information abroad is within the Act if:

- it is going within the European Economic Area;
- the country it is going to has adequate Data Protection provision (according to the European Commission);
- the recipient organisation in the USA has signed up to 'Safe Harbors';
- the interests of the Data Subject are protected by an approved contract;
- you have the consent of the Data Subject;
- it is necessary in connection with a contract involving the Data Subject;
- it complies with a limited number of other circumstances.

Chapter 16

Freedom of Information

The Freedom of Information Act 2000, which came into force on 1 January 2005, is about open government. It is primarily a means of increasing transparency in official decision making and procedures, and enabling citizens to hold government to account.

This chapter:

- Describes the main points of the Freedom of Information Act 2000
- Discusses how voluntary organisations might be able to use the Act to obtain information for campaigning or policy work
- Examines the situations where voluntary organisations may have to provide information under the Freedom of Information Act

Freedom of Information is often mentioned in the same breath as Data Protection. The two pieces of legislation do relate to each other, but only in a limited way. Their starting points are totally different: Data Protection is about protecting individuals; Freedom of Information is about promoting open government. Essentially, the Freedom of Information Act provides a mechanism by which anyone (anywhere in the world, potentially) can ask to see any information held by a public authority, in order to hold that authority to account.

The Freedom of Information Act therefore applies directly only to 'public authorities'. The Act establishes a list of public authorities, and makes provision for organisations to be added to or removed from the list as required.[41] While most of the organisations

---

41 Information on which organisations are covered by the Freedom of Information Act can be found at www.foi.gov.uk/yourRights/coverageguide.htm

on the list are clearly part of government, some might be thought of as within, or on the fringes of, the voluntary sector – such as the Community Development Foundation or the National Consumer Council.

It also provides for two other categories of public authority. These are:

■ bodies not eligible for the main list, but which are designated by the Secretary of State because they are exercising 'functions of a public nature' or 'providing under a contract made with a public authority any service whose provision is a function of that authority' (s.5 of the Act);

■ publicly owned companies (s.6 of the Act).

No voluntary organisations – in fact no organisations at all – have (at the time of writing) been designated under s.5, and the Freedom of Information website (see footnote 41) states that:

> The vast majority of charities are not covered by the Freedom of Information Act [because] almost all charities were established as private organisations . . . The source of their funding is not relevant to whether or not they are covered by the Freedom of Information Act.

> It is theoretically possible that some charities exist which are 'wholly owned' by . . . an organisation which is subject to the Freedom of Information Act. In this case, those charities would also be subject to the Act. However, we are not presently aware of any which do fit this description.

This is slightly misinformed, however, as there are certainly some charities on the list. The Tate Gallery, to take just one example, is an exempt charity. It is also a non-departmental public body and a public authority for the purposes of the Freedom of Information Act.[42]

Note that an organisation cannot be designated without consultation, either with the organisation itself or with someone who 'appears' to represent it.

Using the Act to obtain information

Subject to important exemptions, anyone can ask to see any information held by a public authority. The main exemptions are as follows.

■ Information that would cost too much to provide. There are set limits on the time the authority has to spend in dealing with a request. Below the limit (currently set at around three days' work) there is no charge and the authority must provide the information. Above the limit, the authority may refuse to comply with the request, or may make a charge to cover its costs.

---

42 The Charities Act 2006 in effect abolishes the category of exempt charities by requiring them to register. This provision is expected to come into force in 2009.

- Information specifically about individuals (but incidental information may be included – for example relating to staff of the authority in the course of their work, or where there is a public interest in disclosure, such as when individuals object to a planning application or other similar proposal).

- Information where there is a legal duty of confidentiality, or which is subject to legal professional privilege (or its Scottish equivalent).

- Information that is commercially confidential. This is widely defined as information whose disclosure 'would, or would be likely to, prejudice the commercial interests of any person (including the public authority holding it)'.

- A range of matters where secrecy is paramount, or where revealing the information would be detrimental to the activity, such as national security, defence, international relations, law enforcement, audits and other investigations.

- Information that has to be kept secret until it is announced, such as decisions on the economy.

- Information relating to the formulation of government policy.

Use of the Freedom of Information Act is not restricted to individuals. Voluntary organisations could use it both in their policy work and in their work with individual clients, in order to find out more about the background to policies, procedures and decisions, for example.

Providing information under the Act

When it comes to being required to provide information, one aim of the Act is to encourage public authorities to provide more information as a matter of course. All those to which the Act applies must produce a publication schedule, indicating what information they publish and how to obtain it. If the information requested is already publicly available, the authority does not have to provide it again in response to a Freedom of Information Act request.

There is no charge for a Freedom of Information Act request (unless the provision of the information would exceed the three-day limit, and the authority agrees to provide it at cost). The time limit for a response is 20 working days (i.e. four weeks, against the Data Protection Act Subject Access limit of 40 calendar days).

Voluntary organisations should bear in mind that any information they provide to a public authority – as part of a bidding process, for example – could be disclosed in response to a Freedom of Information request, unless it is clearly exempt, by being commercially confidential, for example.

In such a case the authority does not have to inform the voluntary organisation when information is being disclosed, although some are providing a general warning that disclosure might happen. Where information is intended to be confidential or is felt to be commercially sensitive, it would often be wise to indicate this at the time it is provided to a public authority, so that this can be taken into account in deciding whether to disclose it.

The Act might also catch voluntary organisations through its provision that '... information is held by a public authority if ... it is held by another person on behalf of the authority'. It is possible to imagine a situation where a service is contracted out and the authority, in responding to a Freedom of Information request, requires the voluntary organisation to provide relevant parts of the information it holds in relation to that service. (In this case, however, the information is still being 'held' by the public authority, so the request would have to come via the authority, not directly to the voluntary organisation.) It would be reasonable to expect authorities to specify in their contract terms if they believe any of the information held or generated in relation to the service provided would be subject to Freedom of Information access.

Because Freedom of Information disclosure has to meet the very tight 20-working-day timetable, you should ensure that any information held in your organisation which might be subject to Freedom of Information can be supplied very promptly if required.

Information relating to individuals

The Freedom of Information Act added an additional category of Personal Data to the Data Protection Act, extending its provisions to unstructured data held in manual files by a public authority. Citizens can therefore obtain information about themselves which is held in unstructured paper files – which they would not have access to under a Data Protection Act request to a commercial or voluntary organisation – provided it is not exempt under any of the provisions listed on pages 113 and 114. (There is, however, an exemption for personnel files. The staff of public authorities cannot obtain access to unstructured records about themselves.)

Where an individual wants access to such information about themselves, they make a Subject Access application under the Data Protection Act, not a Freedom of Information Act request. (In practice, however, it makes little difference; provided the request is made in writing, the public authority is bound to respond.)

Information about public officials and others, even when it is Personal Data, may also be disclosed if the public interest takes precedence. For example, the details of expenses paid to senior council staff have been disclosed in response to a Freedom of Information Act request. The Information Tribunal has also ruled that it would be permissible to disclose the names of individuals who had attended events or corporate hospitality organised by a public authority.[43] Normally, however, Personal Data is only available to the Data Subject.

---

43 Information Tribunal Appeal Number: EA/2007/0058.

Summary

- Voluntary organisations may be able to use the Freedom of Information Act to obtain information useful to their work.

- The Freedom of Information Act does not apply directly to most voluntary organisations in terms of being required to provide information.

- Voluntary organisations should be aware that information they provide to public authorities may be liable to disclosure.

- There may be situations where information held by a voluntary organisation on behalf of a public authority (in relation to a contracted-out service, for example) has to be passed to the authority in order to meet a Freedom of Information request.

- Because of the Freedom of Information Act, an individual making a Subject Access request to a public authority may be able to obtain access to information held in unstructured manual files, which would not be available from a commercial or voluntary organisation.

Chapter 17

Confidentiality

Data Protection and confidentiality overlap to a large extent, but do not cover exactly the same material. In most organisations it makes sense to have an overall approach to confidentiality and, within that, to comply with Data Protection law. Clarity over the extent of confidentiality is an important precursor for setting appropriate Data Protection controls.

This chapter:

- Explores the interaction between Data Protection and confidentiality
- Discusses the elements of a confidentiality policy
- Explains when the need to disclose information may override any Data Protection restrictions

We have seen in Chapter 3 that Data Protection law only applies to 'Personal Data', whose definition may exclude information which would normally need to be kept confidential. A wide variety of confidential material may not be Personal Data.

- Verbal information that is not recorded anywhere cannot be data, however personal it might be – a conversation with a client or a colleague, or something overheard, for example.
- Information that is recorded on paper but not in a 'relevant filing system' is not data, even if it is about an identifiable individual (unless it is held by a public authority).
- Information that is not personal may still be confidential – relating to the plans, proposals, negotiations and business practices of the organisation, for example.
- Security information, such as passwords and access codes, is also quite likely not to be personal, but is certainly confidential.

To avoid confusion by having some aspects of confidentiality dealt with under the Data Protection policy and others in a separate policy (or by having the Data Protection policy extend into areas which are not strictly the concern of data protection), it makes sense in most organisations to have a self-standing confidentiality policy which refers to Data Protection when appropriate.

What should a confidentiality policy be based on?

Confidentiality is not the same as secrecy. It is about setting clear boundaries within which information may legitimately be shared on a need-to-know basis. The boundaries will depend partly on the nature of the information, and partly on your policy decisions.

Once boundaries have been set, all parties need to know the situation. If you tell your clients that you offer a confidential service, you should aim to ensure that they are clear what this means: will you keep the information within just the team that is working with them, or within the organisation, or might you even share it with an external professional, such as a GP or social worker? Your staff – paid or volunteer – also need to be clear where the boundaries are: can they share a particular type of information in a particular way as a matter of routine, or do they need to go back to the client to clear the proposed disclosure?

Similarly, you need to be clear with staff, volunteers, donors and others about the extent of confidentiality you are offering. For example, even with a relatively uncontroversial set of data, such as contact people in other organisations, you need to be clear whether you will use the contact details just for your own purposes, whether you will give the details out on a case-by-case basis, or whether you will make them public in some way.

The level of confidentiality will be determined in most cases by three factors:

- any legal responsibilities you have;
- your assessment of the risk posed by sharing the information;
- your decision on how much control over use of the information it is appropriate to give to the individual.

A legal responsibility to maintain confidentiality may be imposed by law, explicitly or implicitly under a contract, or by a professional relationship – counselling, for example.[44]

---

44 See *The Russell-Cooke Voluntary Sector Legal Handbook*, published by the Directory of Social Change, for more detail on the legal aspects of this chapter.

When does a duty to disclose override confidentiality?

It is important not to promise confidentiality when you cannot deliver on that promise. You may have no choice about disclosing information, for a variety of reasons.

You may have a duty of care not to overlook something that comes to your attention. Many advisers, for example, make it clear to their clients that information may be disclosed if the adviser becomes aware of a risk of harm either to the client or to another person (especially a child), even though the relationship is normally based on confidentiality.

Increasingly, funders such as local authorities impose (or try to impose) a contractual obligation to disclose information about the people benefiting from the service. If you agree to funding on these terms, you must ensure that you can do so while complying with the Data Protection Act.

There may be a legal obligation to disclose information. This can come in two forms: a requirement to provide information if asked (which can be dealt with on a case-by-case basis), and – more rarely – a requirement to report information if you become aware of it.

This is not the place to deal with this issue exhaustively, but the number of matters that must be reported, at least in some circumstances, does appear to be growing. Many of these could involve the disclosure of Personal Data. These include, for example:

- employment-related matters to do with tax and national insurance;
- accidents and some breaches of health and safety;
- concerns about potential risk or harm to children or vulnerable adults;
- suspicions relating to terrorism;
- suspicions relating to money laundering;
- suspicions of drug sales and use.

Where there is a duty of confidentiality *without* a legal duty of disclosure, disclosure without the consent of the person to whom the duty of confidentiality is owed could be a breach of confidentiality. In these situations, consent to disclose should be obtained – for example, a counselling client agreeing that the counsellor can discuss him or her in supervision sessions.

Data Protection and breaches of confidentiality

The Data Protection Act allows you to disclose information that you would normally not be allowed to disclose in two cases:

- where another law requires you to make the disclosure;
- where you decide that it is necessary to disclose information in connection with 'crime and taxation' purposes (see overleaf), provided you meet the relevant conditions.

This means that if one of these legal situations applies, you can disclose the information without contravening the Data Protection Act.

It is important to understand that the Act does not give anyone (other than the Data Subject) the right to demand information. Their request must be based on a specific legal power in some other legislation. Many agencies do have the power to demand information, but it is quite reasonable to expect them to know what powers they have.

You are therefore within your rights to ask them to produce a warrant, for example, or to specify in writing exactly which powers they are using, and to demonstrate that the person asking is authorised to do so. The request should also be restricted to clearly identifiable individuals. 'Fishing trips' – where someone asks for information about a lot of people with no real suspicions – are almost certainly outside the powers of most agencies.

The 'crime and taxation' provisions of the Data Protection Act, equally, do not require you to help the police or customs and excise authorities, for example. They say that if you choose to help them you are not in breach of certain Data Protection Principles. The ones you are allowed to break in making the disclosure are:

- the part of the first Data Protection Principle (see Chapter 6) which says that all processing must be fair – but you must still meet at least one of the conditions for fair processing and the conditions for sensitive data, if applicable;
- the Principles (see Chapters 6, 9 and 10) that say you must only use the data for the specified purpose, and that it has to be adequate, relevant, not excessive, accurate, up to date and not held longer than necessary.

Also under this exemption, the Data Subject cannot prevent disclosure under the provision for preventing processing likely to cause damage or distress, and cannot get inaccurate data changed (see Chapter 11).

The 'crime and taxation' purposes are:

- the prevention or detection of crime;
- the apprehension or prosecution of offenders;
- the assessment or collection of any tax or duty.

The exemption can be invoked only if applying the normal rules would be 'likely to prejudice' the purpose.

The Association of Chief Police Officers has agreed a standard form to be used when police are requesting information under the crime and taxation exemptions.[45]

Where you decide to breach confidentiality, either in response to an external request or on your own initiative, you may want to take certain steps to ensure that all the issues are properly considered first. You could:

---

45 Section 29 of the Act.

- insist that any request for information is submitted in writing (with only very rare exceptions in a genuine emergency);

- ask any organisation requesting information to show which legal power it is exercising (not just quoting s.29 or s.35 of the Data Protection Act, which permit disclosure but cannot require it) and, if relevant, the specific authority of the individual making the request;

- release the information only on the authority of an appointed senior member of staff (or trustee);

- keep a record of the disclosure and the reasons for making it.

Privacy

The Human Rights Act 2000 protects individuals' privacy.[46] Several court cases have clarified the extent to which this applies, in particular a case involving the author JK Rowling's son, in 2008. The court of appeal said that if people have a 'reasonable expectation of privacy', then this must be respected. It does not mean that information cannot be published, but that intrusive publication (most cases have revolved around photographs) may be prohibited.

This is a developing area of law, and it is difficult to make specific recommendations. It would be wise, however, to consider carefully before publishing photographs or other information which might breach an individual's privacy, embarrass them or draw unwanted and unjustified attention to them.

Disclosing data in order to protect children and vulnerable adults

Many statutory bodies have a duty to share information about children and vulnerable adults, with the aim of ensuring that no one who is at risk 'falls through the net'.[47]

Voluntary agencies, especially when they are working closely with the statutory sector, are increasingly expected to participate in these information-sharing exercises, even though they are not necessarily subject to exactly the same legislation. For example, the non-statutory guidance *What to do if you're worried a child is being abused*[48] explicitly states that it is for 'those working in the statutory or the independent sector'.

---

46 Although the Human Rights Act only applies directly to statutory bodies, the courts must interpret other legislation in the light of the Act. It is this which is gradually extending its application more generally.
47 In the 'Climbié case' in 2000, several agencies were aware of potential problems, but no one agency had the complete picture, and none therefore took the matter seriously enough. Victoria Climbié died at the hands of her family as a result.
48 Department for Education and Skills, 2006, ISBN: 978–1-84478–867–5, also available at www.teacher net.gov.uk, document reference: 04320–2006DOM-EN.

The document is based on the Children Act 2004 and mainly describes child protection procedures, but there is also a section specifically on information sharing. This makes no explicit reference to the Data Protection Act. There is no suggestion that the Act would ever prevent you from sharing information where this is the right thing to do – even where this means breaking confidentiality. Indeed, it would be perverse for a piece of legislation which is fundamentally about protecting people to prevent you from acting appropriately.

The guidance does, however, put information sharing in the context of confidentiality and it sets out good practice – including informing the child and/or family and getting their consent where appropriate, ensuring that the data is accurate and relevant, taking advice when in doubt and documenting your decisions and actions. In other words, complying with the Data Protection Principles.

This is a good example of the correct approach: do the right thing, but do it carefully and in a way which fully takes account of your Data Protection responsibilities.

Your confidentiality policy

A confidentiality policy should recognise that confidentiality is about boundaries, not total secrecy. It should be clear about:

- *who* (usually by role, rather than as an individual) has access to *which information*, and for what *purpose(s)*;
- whether access is automatic, or needs to be authorised in each case, or in specific cases (such as where information is especially confidential);
- any likely exceptions to the confidentiality undertaking;
- how Data Subjects will be informed about the confidentiality policy, and in particular any exceptions to confidentiality;
- how Data Subjects will be consulted over disclosures of confidential information, and how their consent, if given, will be recorded;
- how staff, and anyone else who has access to confidential information, will be informed and trained on their responsibilities regarding confidentiality;
- how disclosures that the organisation decides to make which breach confidentiality will be handled and authorised;
- the penalties for breaches of confidentiality by individual staff members without the organisation's authority;
- any related policies (such as security or whistle-blowing, for example).

In support of the full policy, you may also want to have specific documents for your main Data Subjects and for staff.

For Data Subjects it is often useful to have a brief privacy or confidentiality statement which is made available to all clients (and others whose information will be held confidentially). This does not need to go into all the details, but should give the bare bones – that information will be held confidentially within the organisation (or within a specific team) and not normally disclosed – and indicate where further detail can be found. This may be a more detailed document, or you may direct people to a member of staff, for example.

The same policy should also be used on your website, possibly with additions to refer to web-specific issues such as the use of cookies. There should be no real difference in the treatment of information collected on paper, face to face, by phone or on the web, and therefore the same confidentiality statement should apply to all media.

Many organisations also find it useful to have a brief summary of the confidentiality responsibilities of staff, volunteers and others who have access to confidential information. Newcomers to your organisation, or people moving into a new role, should sign a copy of this statement to indicate that they have received and understood it. Any breach of confidentiality can then be treated as a disciplinary matter, if necessary. However, a statement on its own is not enough, even if signed. You must also ensure that you cover confidentiality during induction and training programmes, so that staff have the opportunity to clarify any uncertainties and so that you can be confident that they have understood how you expect them to behave.

In addition to this, staff themselves, of course, are your Data Subjects, and you may want to include something in your staff handbook setting out how you treat their information confidentially and your procedures for making disclosures (either at the employee or volunteer's request, or in response to an official request).

Summary

- Confidentiality usually extends beyond the Personal Data which is subject to the Data Protection Act.
- Confidentiality is about setting clear boundaries, and making sure that all involved understand them.
- Confidentiality can rarely be absolute. The law requires certain disclosures to be made – in some cases when you become aware of the information, but more usually on request from an official agency.
- Disclosures required by law, or for 'crime and taxation' purposes, are not a breach of Data Protection as long as they are properly made.
- Your full confidentiality policy may need to be supported by statements for specific types of Data Subject and guidance for members of staff or volunteers who have access to confidential information.

Examples

1) Luis is visiting a client at her home. As soon as he arrives, she says angrily, 'You told me everything we talked about was confidential. How come my social worker knows what we were discussing last week?' Luis remembers having a phone conversation with the social worker, because he wanted to make sure social services was aware that the client's situation had recently changed. He realises that he didn't specifically mention this to the client.

   He apologises to the client and explains what had happened. After a while she accepts his apology. When he gets back to the office he raises it at a team meeting. The case notes say that the confidentiality policy was explained to the client by her original case worker at the very first meeting with her, but this was some time ago, and no one can remember which version of the confidentiality policy applied at the time. She might not have been told that her social worker might be contacted.

   In any case, the team agrees to review its practice. First, it changes the policy, so that all contacts with social services – even apparently 'trivial' ones – only take place after the client has been told, unless there is a very good reason not to. It also agrees that it would be good practice to remind clients what the confidentiality policy says, once a year.

2) Wally is a youth worker. He is having difficulties with a particular young person who has a complicated home life. The young person's parents are also involved. Not having anyone at work to talk things through with, Wally confides in his wife, who is a teacher and has some experience of this sort of thing. She helps him decide on his course of action, and he sorts everything out just before going on holiday.

   On their way back from holiday, Wally's wife bumps into the young person's mother at the airport, and expresses her sympathy for the situation, only to find out that the parents had recently split up, the young person is living with the father and his new partner, and the mother knew nothing about the problems.

   Clearly this is a serious breach of confidentiality. Wally immediately reports it to his boss, who commends him for owning up so promptly. The boss says she understands the temptation to discuss work problems with a partner whose judgement is trusted and who can perhaps be more objective, but Wally should never have identified the individuals concerned to anyone outside the organisation. He promises not to do it again and the boss agrees to apologise to the family and try to smooth things over. She also agrees to try to set up a better system so that in future staff in Wally's situation can talk difficult problems through with a colleague.

Chapter 18

E-mail and the web

Although there is nothing intrinsically different about applying the Data Protection rules to the use of e-mail and the web, it is useful to consider in one place the issues affecting electronic communication.

This chapter:

- Reviews all the Data Protection issues affecting the use of e-mail and the web
- Takes into account the Lawful Business Practice Regulations and the European E-Commerce Directive

Protecting the contents of e-mails

E-mails are in many cases legally equivalent to paper documents. Even ordinary e-mails can be regarded as contractual documents, and a name typed at the bottom of an e-mail is often as good as a signature. Further developments with systems to authenticate e-mails (i.e. to ensure they come from the person they purport to come from and have not been tampered with en route) can only hasten this development.[49]

Since January 2007 the rules[50] have been clarified to make it clear that many e-mails count as 'business letters' and must therefore include any information that is required to be given on other business documents (such as company and charity registration details). Similarly, as with other documents, e-mails may contain libels or commit the organisation to contractual terms or constitute sexual or other forms of harassment. There have been several well-publicised court cases in which organisations had to pay substantial damages as a result of comments or statements made by employees in e-mails.

---

49 See, for example, European Directive 99/93/EC, the Electronic Signatures Directive, implemented in the UK through the Electronic Signatures Regulations 2002, SI 2002 No. 318.
50 The most recent legislation in respect of companies, at the time of writing, is the Companies (Trading Disclosures) Regulations 2008, in force from 1 October 2008.

If an e-mail includes information about an identifiable living individual, this constitutes Personal Data and could lead to the individual being harmed if the information were to get into the wrong hands. While mentioning a person by name is not necessarily a problem, transmitting confidential information about a client, for example, would require considerably more care. It should be remembered that, just as with telephone lines, many users, both at home and at work, share their e-mail accounts. You cannot necessarily assume that an e-mail sent to a particular address will be read only by the addressee unless you have established with them that this is a secure method of contacting them.

Many organisations try to limit their liability by inserting disclaimers automatically at the bottom of every e-mail sent from their organisation.[51] The consensus among practitioners appears to be that disclaimers at the bottom of an e-mail intended to secure confidentiality (on the lines of 'If you receive this in error, let us know and don't read it') are unlikely to be effective – if for no other reason than that the recipient has read the whole e-mail before they get to the disclaimer. Disclaimers intended to restrict an organisation's liability for the contents (to the effect that the views expressed are those of the sender personally, not the organisation, or that the e-mail is not intended to create a contract) may be worth considering, provided they are not attached automatically when the organisation genuinely wants to make a commitment.

Instead of using a confidentiality disclaimer, it is better to take specific measures to improve the confidentiality of the contents of e-mails, where necessary. These could include:

- taking care to establish that an e-mail address is correct, before using it to send confidential materials;

- enclosing confidential material as an attachment, so that the body of the e-mail can instruct unintended recipients not to read the attachment;

- better still, using password protection on the attached document, and communicating the password to the recipient through other means. (Such passwords can be reasonably easily broken, but should be enough to deter access by people who receive the e-mail in error rather than by deliberate interception);

- employing user-transparent encryption (i.e. methods for 'scrambling' the data at one end and 'unscrambling' it at the other that do not impinge on the ordinary user) when transferring confidential information between organisations (or parts of organisations) that are regularly in contact.

E-mail addresses

There is a debate over whether e-mail addresses on their own should be regarded as Personal Data under the Data Protection Act. One side believes that an e-mail address

---

51 It is not the place of this book to give technical details of how to operate e-mail systems. None of the ideas discussed here are technically complicated, and all should be possible using any e-mail system.

in itself constitutes Personal Data if it is specific to the person concerned, even if the content of the address doesn't identify the individual directly. For example, 'johnking@ourorganisation.org.uk' would be Personal Data; 'johnk453@isp.net' might be Personal Data; but 'info@ourorganisation.org.uk' would not.

In the past, the Information Commissioner has sometimes appeared to take the view that the e-mail address is not Personal Data until it is linked with other information held by the Data Controller. Clearly an e-mail address that formed part of a set of contact details for an individual would be Personal Data. However, the legal guidance (issued soon after the Act came into force) is clear. It says that:

> In the context of the Internet, many e-mail addresses are Personal Data where the e-mail address clearly identifies a particular individual. The Commissioner is Elizabeth France. The e-mail address elizabethfrance@dataprotection.gov.uk is thus Personal Data about the Commissioner.

Guidance for individuals on their rights, issued in 2000, however, does not make this distinction. It says bluntly that:

> E-mail addresses are Personal Data. If you find yourself on a directory or user list you can request to be omitted from it.

A pragmatic approach is probably worth taking. Even in those cases where e-mail addresses may not technically be Personal Data, inappropriate disclosure will almost certainly cause irritation and can potentially cause harm. As a matter of good practice they should therefore be treated responsibly.

One of the commonest ways in which e-mail addresses are inappropriately disclosed is where you are sending the same e-mail to a group of people and put all the addresses in the 'To' or 'Cc' fields. This allows all the recipients to acquire each other's addresses. In some cases – with a group of people working closely together, for example – this might be appropriate and desirable, but in many cases it is poor practice. Putting the addresses in the 'Bcc' field is usually enough to avoid the disclosure. (However, some users block incoming mail sent as 'blind' copies in an attempt to reduce unsolicited marketing by e-mail.) For regular mailings, a more robust solution is to use a mail server, so that the sender just mails the message to the particular list and the server takes care of delivering it without disclosing the whole group's addresses to everyone else.

Since a Data Subject does not have to be in the UK, any e-mail addresses of overseas contacts could also be Personal Data and subject to the Data Protection Act. Transferring Personal Data outside the UK is subject to the restrictions in the eighth Data Protection Principle. If the address is sent to a country without adequate Data Protection, the transfer must meet an appropriate condition. The most likely are as follows.

- Where the transfer is necessary in connection with a contract the Data Subject is party to, or which is in their interests. You could probably use this to require your staff to allow their work e-mail addresses to be used where their work requires them to have contact from overseas. However, a preferable alternative is to use generic addresses wherever possible for general use: 'info@ourorganisation.org.uk' rather than 'smith.j@ourorganisation.org.uk', for example.

■ Where the Data Subject has consented to the transfer. Consent must be 'specific, informed and freely given' in the same way as consent as a condition for fair processing.

Monitoring staff e-mails

There are many dangers for an organisation if staff misuse e-mails – not just from the Data Protection perspective. Other problems result if careless use results in malicious software being allowed in, or if over-use for private purposes starts to have a noticeable impact on the performance of the staff member.

Many organisations therefore feel the need to monitor staff e-mails to prevent malicious, deliberate or inadvertent misuse. However, monitoring communications in these circumstances is outlawed by the Regulation of Investigatory Powers Act 2000, unless it meets conditions set out in the Lawful Business Practice Regulations.[52] In addition, everyone has a reasonable expectation of privacy under the Human Rights Act. The Lawful Business Practice Regulations, in essence, allow any business – which includes voluntary organisations – to monitor or keep a record of electronic communications (such as phone calls or e-mails) in order to check that no one is misusing the system or doing anything illegal, and for quality control purposes. The main restriction is that you must make 'all reasonable efforts' to inform all users of the system that their communications may be intercepted.

Blanket monitoring and arbitrary intrusion into privacy are not permitted. It is likely to be acceptable to monitor traffic – to note how many e-mails an employee sends or receives, for example – but you must have a good reason to open and read specific e-mails. If you are going to do this, you *must* make the ground rules clear to your staff and, as far as possible, to people from outside communicating with you.

The Information Commissioner recommends that monitoring, where it does take place, should be automated as far as possible, to minimise the amount of intrusion into the contents of e-mails. The implications of all this legislation are discussed in more detail by the Commissioner in the Code of Practice on Employment Records (see Chapter 22).

---

52 SI 2000 No. 2699 The Telecommunications (Lawful Business Practice) (Interception of Communications) Regulations 2000.

Acceptable Use Policies

If you decide to have an Acceptable Use Policy it should explain clearly:

- what your organisation regards as acceptable use of e-mail and the web;
- which breaches will be counted as gross misconduct;
- what monitoring and enforcement action may be taken.

You need to leave as little as possible open to interpretation. Your idea of 'occasional' private use may be very different from someone else's. It is quite usual for every employee and volunteer to be required to sign the policy, and give their consent to the monitoring, before being allowed to use e-mail or the web.

Heavy-handed monitoring is hard to justify and counter-productive, but if you have an explicit policy it is easier to take action when you need to. Don't forget that people have rights to privacy. Reading their e-mails is as much of an intrusion as checking up on how often they go to the lavatory or stare out of the window 'thinking'.

In an Acceptable Use Policy you may wish to:

- specify how much personal use of e-mail and web access is allowed, if any. (For example: 'You may use the Internet for legitimate work-related purposes only. Personal use is not allowed' or 'Urgent personal e-mails can be sent, provided this is in your own time and does not interfere with your work');
- state any restrictions on staff use of social networking sites from work;
- set out how staff can maintain the privacy of any private e-mails (for example by putting them in a separate folder), while making it clear that total privacy is not possible;
- ban private use of the e-mail system for commercial purposes or bulk mailings;
- ban harassment and the sending, forwarding or viewing on the web of defamatory or offensive material and make it clear that these could constitute gross misconduct;
- ban the sending of e-mails in the name of someone else and make it clear that this could constitute gross misconduct;
- give guidance on the appropriate content and format of work e-mails (including making sure that your organisation is properly identified and that all legally required information is included);
- give guidance on how to maintain confidentiality, as suggested above;
- explain that the employer reserves the right to monitor use of e-mail and the web;
- set out the circumstances in which monitoring will be undertaken to detect or investigate breaches of the policy, and who may authorise it or carry it out;
- explain the circumstances in which a person's e-mail will be accessed for business reasons – for example when they are on holiday or absent for other reasons.

It is worth thinking carefully about what you put into your Acceptable Use Policy and how you monitor it. A survey[53] in 2008 claimed that nearly half (44%) of UK companies had fired workers during the previous year because of abuses of e-mail.

Collecting Personal Data on a website

In some ways, information collected over the Internet requires more care, and the Data Subjects require more reassurance, than in more traditional settings. If you are based in the UK, or if any of the Personal Data is processed in the UK, then UK Data Protection law applies, even if your Data Subjects are on the other side of the world.

You will need a privacy or confidentiality statement unless your website is merely used for publishing information, and doesn't collect any feedback or information from users (with or without their knowledge). Most of the information in it will be similar to the information you have to provide on printed material (see following chapter), but other aspects are specific to the Internet. The statement (or more specific material at appropriate places on your website) should contain information about:

- who the data is being collected for (the identity of the Data Controller);
- what Personal Data is being collected, both overtly and covertly;
- which of the data being asked for is optional. (Often mandatory fields will be indicated with an asterisk, or shown in a different colour);
- what purposes the data is being collected for, and in particular whether the information is to be used for marketing;
- whether the Data Subject is being asked to consent to use of the data for specific purposes, with provision to indicate that consent, and whether they can opt out of any uses – especially marketing;
- where the data might be transferred or disclosed to (with an option to opt out unless the transfer or disclosure is necessary to the primary purpose);
- what rights the Data Subject has with respect to the data (for example access, correction and deletion) and how they can be exercised;
- how long the data will be kept;
- what security measures are in place, especially where the Data Subject is being asked to part with information, such as credit card details;
- whether anonymous browsing is possible;
- the site policy on cookies and Internet Protocol (IP) addresses;[54]

---

53 For e-mail security firm Proofpoint, carried out by Forrester and reported at Out-law.com 29/05/2008.
54 In other words, whether the website will collect information about the user in ways they may not be aware of. The IP address tells a website how to locate your computer, so that it can send back the web pages you have asked to view. This information does not necessarily identify you personally but, in some circumstances, it could allow a website to monitor your browsing habits. Regulation 6 of the Privacy and Electronic Communications Regulations 2003 requires that users must be informed if cookies are being used.

- a reminder that linked sites may have different privacy practices (unless you are prepared to vouch for the sites you link to);
- who should be contacted for more information.

The Information Commissioner's guidance[55] suggests that the privacy statement should be accessible from all pages on your site, not just the home page (since people may not enter the site there), and that a 'layered' approach is preferable. If you have a full notice, with a lot of legal provisions, you should also have a condensed notice with the main information and alerts at appropriate places to direct people to the more detailed information.

The Commissioner also suggests that if you 'harvest' personal information from the web, even if it has been made available by, or with the knowledge of, the individual, you are not necessarily allowed to use it in unfair ways. You should, therefore, think carefully about whether your proposed use is fair in the context of how and why the information was made public. For example, it would almost certainly not be acceptable to use e-mail addresses or phone numbers for marketing if they were the personal details of individuals who are volunteer local group contacts, and whose contact information has been published so that people can make contact with a voluntary organisation.

Another consideration, covered in the Commissioner's guidance, is that you cannot change your privacy statement retrospectively. In other words, if you gave people certain assurances at the time you collected their information, then you must stick to those. Your new conditions can only apply to people whose data you collect after you have changed your statement.

If your website is aimed at children or young people, the material on it – including privacy statements – should be aimed at their level of understanding.

Publishing personal information on your website

One of the defining characteristics of the web is that it is 'world wide'. This means that any information on your site could be transferred abroad and, by extension, could be going to countries that do not have adequate Data Protection provisions (see Chapter 15).

There is some uncertainty about the exact legal position, because a European Court of Justice case in 2003[56] found that: 'given the state of development of the Internet at the time the directive was drawn up . . . the Community legislature did not intend the expression "transfer of data to a third country" to cover the loading of data onto an Internet page even if such data are thereby made accessible to persons in third countries'.

---

55 *Good Practice Note: Collecting personal information using websites.*
56 Case C-101/01, which upheld the conviction of a Swede, Bodil Lindqvist, who was fined about £300 for processing Personal Data of her church group by putting information about members onto a web page without their knowledge or permission, but was held not to have transferred it abroad.

It is by no means certain, however, that this ruling applies to all websites – especially if they are public rather than directed specifically to a restricted group. You should probably, therefore, regard any publicly available website as potentially involving a transfer abroad, and this means that you should consider whether you provide the security envisaged in the eighth Data Protection Principle or meet any of the conditions in Schedule 4 which allow you to transfer data without protection. In practice, in most cases the only available option is likely to be Data Subject consent.

This means that you should think twice before you publish Personal Data on your website. Remember that Personal Data in this context can include photographs, because they are being processed automatically, as well as the more obvious written information about the Data Subject. If you want to publish Personal Data on your site, you should normally only do so with the consent of the Data Subject.

When seeking consent, in order for it to be 'informed' you probably need to make it clear to the Data Subject that their information is potentially going to countries where it will not have the same level of protection as in the UK.

In a few cases you may decide that you do not need consent. These might include the following examples.

- Occasionally, you may be able to argue that it is necessary to put the data on your site in connection with a contract involving the Data Subject, or for their benefit, but remember it must be *necessary*, if you want to publish without consent. There are usually likely to be alternative ways of achieving your ends.
- If access to your site is restricted (and your security measures work) you may be able to ensure that the data only goes to people in countries with adequate Data Protection, or who have signed an appropriate contract with you.
- You may decide that where information is already in the public domain (for example the author's name on a book), transferring it abroad without protection is acceptable.

All these situations should be treated with care, however. You may be in contact with people who are perfectly happy for their details to be available in this country, but who have reasons for not wanting them to be readily available abroad – perhaps in a country they have had to flee as a refugee. Consent is by far the safest route, if you need to put Personal Data on your website at all.

Using the Internet to sell products or raise funds

The European E-commerce Directive (00/31/EC) was agreed on 8 June 2000.[57] This covers 'information society services'. These are described, in short, as 'services normally

---

57 And was put into UK law under the Electronic Commerce (EC Directive) Regulations 2002 (SI 2002 No. 2013).

provided for remuneration, at a distance, by means of electronic equipment for the processing and storage of data and at the individual request of a recipient of a service'. It includes services provided free of charge to the recipient (for example funded by advertising) and online direct marketing and advertising. The regulations clearly apply to online sales and marketing, whether for products or services, and almost certainly to online membership recruitment. It is not clear whether they apply to online fundraising, but it would be prudent – and good practice – to apply the principles in the regulations to *all* online financial transactions.

The parts of the regulations that are most relevant here are those requiring transparency and the provisions for concluding a contract electronically.

Assuming that your organisation is the service provider, you must ensure that you 'make available' to the recipient 'in a form and manner which is easily, directly and permanently accessible', among other things:

- the organisation's name and official address;
- contact details, including an e-mail address, that allow you to be contacted 'rapidly', 'directly' and 'effectively';
- details of your registration in any 'trade or similar register'. This could presumably include charity registration details;
- your VAT number, if applicable.

As well as providing e-mail contact details, it is good practice to provide a phone number so that people have an alternative means of contacting you or checking your bona fides.

'Commercial communications' (essentially, marketing material, but probably excluding charity fundraising e-mails) must be identified as such, and if unsolicited marketing is sent by e-mail, it must be 'clearly and unambiguously identifiable as such as soon as it is received'. This could be taken to mean that the subject line of any marketing e-mail must indicate that it contains marketing material.

Where the whole transaction takes place electronically, you must, among other things:

- make the process clear, comprehensible and unambiguous so that the user knows that they are entering a contract, and knows how to check it and amend the details before confirming the transaction;
- allow them to keep a copy of any terms and conditions;
- acknowledge receipt of any order without undue delay, and by electronic means.

If you fail to comply, a contract will not be valid and you may have to compensate the user.

This is only a brief résumé of the regulations. Further information is available on the website of the Department for Business Innovation & Skills (previously Business Enterprise & Regulatory Reform).

There is some debate about where this leaves 'spam' – unsolicited marketing by e-mail. Clearly if someone has opted out of marketing, then you must not approach them in any way, including by e-mail. Some commentators would go further, and argue that unsolicited e-mail is, in effect, outlawed by a combination of European Directives. Others, pointing to the fact that e-mail is regulated by the E-commerce Directive, make the case that you wouldn't need to regulate something if it were illegal.

None of this, of course, can have any effect on spam originating from outside countries not covered by European or equivalent legislation, but for UK-based organisations it is worth being cautious. Many are now adopting an opt-in procedure for e-mail communication. Clearly if someone has consented in advance to being contacted by e-mail there is unlikely to be a problem.

Selling over the Internet (as well as by mail order, for example) is also subject to the Consumer Protection (Distance Selling) Regulations 2000.[58] These apply to trans-actions with consumers (i.e. not business to business) and provide, among other things, a cooling off period of seven working days after the order has been taken.

Summary

- You must make sure that your organisation follows good practice in the composition and distribution of e-mails, in order to achieve transparency and confidentiality.

- You should be careful not to disclose e-mail addresses unnecessarily or inadvertently.

- There are limits on the extent to which you can monitor staff e-mails and use of the internet, especially if you do this without telling them.

- Many organisations find it worth setting out an Acceptable Use Policy for staff use of the Internet while at work.

- You are very likely to have to produce e-mails concerning the Data Subject in response to a Subject Access request.

- You must ensure that your website provides users with the required information before seeking to collect any information from or about them.

- Publishing Personal Data on your website (including photographs) almost certainly needs consent.

- Online marketing, selling and fundraising must take account of the E-Commerce Regulations.

- Many commentators recommend obtaining permission for regular contacts by e-mail, such as electronic newsletters, while unsolicited e-mail marketing is unlawful without prior consent from the recipient.

---

58 These Regulations implement the Distance Selling Directive 97/7/EC.

Chapter 19

Providing the Data Subject with information

Previous chapters have discussed various situations in which the Data Subject needs to be provided with information and, frequently, offered opt-out options.

This chapter:

- Draws these situations together
- Gives examples of Data Protection statements

A balance has to be struck between the clear requirement to ensure that a Data Subject has the information they are entitled to and the danger of overloading people with unhelpful detail. This is particularly true if your initial contact with people is while they are under stress, or if there are other reasons why they may not be capable of taking in the implications of a Data Protection statement.

The rule of thumb is to ask: 'Have we done enough to ensure that the Data Subject is unlikely to get any surprises from our use of the data (including any disclosure we might make to other people) at any stage?'

As described in Chapter 6, there is certain basic information that all Data Subjects must have. This includes being aware of which organisation is holding data about them for what purpose(s), what types of disclosure may be made, and how to exercise their rights.

You could consider:

- a standard short statement on your leaflets and forms;
- a standard paragraph in letters welcoming new members, donors or clients;

- an occasional short piece in your newsletter;
- a privacy statement on your website;
- a notice in your waiting room;
- a standard piece in any telephone scripts;
- notices in contracts – of employment, for example.

Note that the Act says only that you need to ensure that the Data Subject has the information available to them, not that you have to tell them explicitly. So if they already know, or if it is obvious, you need do nothing.

> **Do we have to state on our notepaper, etc., that we are registered under the Data Protection Act?**
>
> No. There is no point. You are bound by the Act whether you have 'notified' (the new term for registration) or not.

Data Protection statements

When you are inserting a Data Protection statement in any document, the following checklist covers some of the main considerations.

- Say who you are and the purpose(s) for which you want the data.
- Identify possible disclosures to other organisations or transfers abroad.
- Offer an opt-out from disclosure to other organisations if this is appropriate, or explain the circumstances in which disclosure will happen.
- Offer an opt-out from direct marketing, if relevant.
- Indicate any data items on the form that are voluntary.
- Explain explicitly why you need any sensitive data for which you are asking.
- Be 'fair'. Provide as much information as necessary about how you will use the data, including any security measures or self-imposed restrictions that may reassure the Data Subject.

> **Do I have to tell people that their data is going on to a computer?**
>
> No. This was only relevant under the 1984 Act, which applied only to computerised records.

You may decide that, instead of a single Data Protection statement, it is more appropriate to put the relevant information in different places within the document. This is completely acceptable. The test is whether the Data Subject ends up with the right information. You do not even need to refer to the term 'Data Protection', unless you think it will help your Data Subjects.

You should also consider having a full, more detailed privacy or Data Protection statement, which can be made available on your website and provided on request in other situations.

Sample privacy/Data Protection statement

The Organisation obtains information about you in the course of its dealings with you. This policy explains how we look after that information and what we do with it.

We have a legal duty under the Data Protection Act to prevent your information falling into the wrong hands. We must also ensure that the data we hold is accurate, adequate, relevant and not excessive.

We do not hold any information about you apart from the information you provide, and our own records of the services we have delivered. The only information our website records automatically is your IP address, so that we can assess which pages are the most popular. These IP addresses aren't linked to any Personal Data so that visitors to our site remain anonymous. We do not send cookies from our website.

We store all your information securely, we restrict access to those who have a need to know, and we train our staff in handling the information securely.

When we telephone you we may ask you certain questions to verify your identity, so that we do not inadvertently disclose information about you to other people, including members of your household. However, we also give you the opportunity to tell us that there are people you don't mind us talking to if this is more convenient.

We do not share your information with any other organisation without your permission.[59] Whenever we collect information which may be used for marketing or fundraising we will inform you of this, and give you the opportunity to opt out.

You have the right to a copy of all the information we hold about you (apart from a very few things which we may be obliged to withhold because they concern other people as well as you). To obtain a copy, write to or e-mail the Data Protection Officer at The Organisation. There is a charge of £10 for a copy of your data (as permitted by law), and we will require proof of your identity. We aim to reply as promptly as we can and, in any case, within the legal maximum of 40 calendar days.

---

59 Note that it is not mandatory to include this provision. If this is in fact your policy, it is worth saying so, but be aware that it may restrict your activities at a later date.

Disproportionate effort

You do not have to provide the Data Subject with information if it would involve 'disproportionate effort'. This is almost the only ground on which information may be withheld. (Others include where the information must by law be processed, or under certain exemptions, discussed on page 140.) This does not mean that you can just decide that it would be too much bother. You must be able to justify this.

The Act does not define disproportionate effort, but the Information Commissioner's legal guidance suggests that a balance has to be struck between the effect on the Data Subject and factors such as the nature of the data and the cost to the Data Controller in providing the information and the time it would take.

Thus, if you acquire details of another voluntary organisation's supporters in order to approach them for money, the effort of making sure that they know who you are and what you are doing, the first time you write, would be minimal. You should therefore tell them (and give them all the information they need about how to exercise their rights – for example to stop you contacting them again).

However, if your contact person in another organisation leaves and says, 'After I've left, talk to Sam if you need anything', you obviously don't need to go to the trouble of phoning Sam and saying, 'By the way, you're now on our database as the contact for this organisation'.

Where you are using information that is already in the public domain, you are much more likely to be able to argue 'disproportionate effort'. Such information might include a list of journalists on your media database, a list of solicitors in a directory or details of professionals such as doctors or social workers who are connected with your clients.

Remember that if you decide not to tell people you are holding their information, you *must* by law keep a record of your reasons for believing that the effort is disproportionate (although this requirement is very widely ignored). A note in your Data Protection policy or a minute of the relevant meeting are likely to be suitable ways of recording this. It is wise to clarify that the decision has been made formally, on behalf of the organisation, not at the whim of an individual.

We carry out profiling of potential major donors before we approach them. Do we now have to tell them we're doing this? That would defeat the purpose.

Here, by definition, you are obtaining the data from a third party. If you are collecting information from the public domain, and provided your intention is to tell the Data Subject eventually, then you can almost certainly justify collecting the information in secret for a reasonable time under 'disproportionate effort'. However, you should be careful to hold the information only for the minimum time necessary before informing the Data Subjects.

You also have to be 'fair' to the Data Subject (including complying with the Conditions in Schedule 2 and, if appropriate, Schedule 3 of the Act), and meet the requirements for good-quality data. If the information is from private, not public, sources, if it is 'sensitive', and if you don't check it carefully, you are much less likely to be compliant with good Data Protection practice.

You can certainly reduce the effort of telling people in many cases. Could you put a notice in your waiting room? You may decide that you don't then need to say anything further in your discussions with clients, service users or visitors. Could you include the information in something you are sending people anyway – a short statement in your newsletter, for example?

You could also make a point of telling people how to find out more if they want to. Prepare a more detailed statement about your activities, as suggested above, which is ready for anyone who asks.

We have lots of people on our database whose details we first collected long ago, before we started taking Data Protection seriously. Do we have to go back to them all now and tell them we have their data?

Almost certainly not. If you are still using the data regularly to keep in touch with them, they already know you have their details, and what you are using the data for. If they haven't been in touch, and you got the data from elsewhere, then you may be able to argue 'disproportionate effort'.

However, you would be very wise to check that you are complying with all the other Principles. Is the data still adequate and relevant? Are you keeping it longer than necessary? Have you told them how to exercise their new opt-out rights – for example through a notice in your newsletter?

Data about third parties

A complication may arise where you collect information about a third party (perhaps another family member, a landlord, or someone the Data Subject is in dispute with) at the same time as getting other information from the Data Subject. In some circumstances, particularly if the information is put on computer, the third party may also be a Data Subject. Do they have to be informed of this, and if so, how?

Where you are fairly sure that the third party is happy with the situation, you are likely to want them to know what is happening. For example, if someone is down as the emergency contact for a child in your care or for a staff member, you have an interest in checking that they know this and have agreed. Otherwise they may not be available when you need them. One way to inform them would be to contact them yourself. A simpler alternative would be that, when you collect the information from the Data Subject, you get them to confirm that they have told the person that their name is being put down, and – if relevant – that they have given their consent.

There may be other cases where you don't want the third party to know you have information about them. Normally you have no option but to inform them. However, see 'disproportionate effort' on page 138 and the exemptions discussed below.

You should also weigh up your Data Protection responsibilities against others, such as health and safety. If there would be a significant risk to your staff, for example, from informing the Data Subject that you held data about them, this would argue against informing them.

Even where the information you hold about third parties is less contentious, you still need to think carefully about how you handle it. For example, where you hold information in your staff files about next of kin, you should tell your staff:

- to inform the individuals that their details have been given as next of kin (so that they don't get a shock if they are ever contacted by you);
- that information on next of kin will only be used strictly in an emergency (and not, for example, for trying to get hold of a holidaying staff member on a business matter, however urgent).

Other subject information exemptions

There are a very few cases where, largely for obvious reasons, the Act says that you do not have to tell the Data Subject about how you are processing their data. For example, if you decide to disclose information to the police in order to help them prevent crime or catch criminals, you do not have to tip off the Data Subject that you have done this.

Another set of exemptions applies to regulatory activity, including 'protecting charities against misconduct or mismanagement . . . protecting the property of charities from loss or misapplication [or] recovery of the property of charities'. Again, if you need to disclose information for these purposes, you do not have to tell the Data Subject if it would 'prejudice the proper discharge' of the activity.

Similar provisions apply in the case of 'securing the health, safety and welfare of persons at work', or where legal professional privilege applies.

These exemptions are not to be used lightly. Usually it is wrong to keep the Data Subject in the dark, but the provisions are there for the rare occasions when they are needed.

Template for an information panel

It is important not to go overboard in providing information. The example opposite is not intended to be a model to be used in full. Rather it is a template, where all the parts in round brackets '( )' have to be filled in with your own information, while the parts in square brackets '[ ]' are optional, to be used only if they apply.

The words can, of course, be adapted to suit your particular audience.

We/(The Data Controller) will use the information you have provided here [and other information you may provide us with in the future] for the purpose[s] of (purposes).

[We will not disclose this information to any other person or organisation, except in connection with the above purposes./We may disclose this information to other [types of] organisations for the purpose of (purpose). If you object to such disclosure, please tick here [   ].]

[Other information required to make the collection fair.]

[If you do not want us to contact you about other [products/services/projects/events/etc.] in future, please tick this box [   ].]

[We may want to contact you in future by telephone about other [products/services/projects/events/etc.]. If you are happy for us to do so, please tick this box [   ].][60]

[We may want to contact you in future by e-mail or text message about other [products/services/projects/events/etc.]. If you are happy for us to do so, please tick this box [   ].]

If you have any query about the use we make of your data, please contact (Data Protection Officer).

[With respect to the data about (sensitive areas) we need this because (details).]

This 'signpost' was produced by the Information Commissioner to offer a consistent and recognisable way of drawing attention to the fact that Personal Data is being collected and to Data Protection statements. For more information (and an option to download the signpost image) see the Information Commissioner's website. The signpost and its intended uses are also described in a leaflet available from the Commissioner.

However, the signpost has not been widely adopted. There is some concern that on websites it might be confused with the padlock symbol indicating a secure connection.

---

60 This statement, and the parallel one on e-mail, represent best practice, ensuring that you have consent for these means of contact. Some commentators feel it is impractical to include them.

Data Protection

Summary

- When you provide information to the Data Subject, make sure that it is prominent, easily identified and easily understood.

- Don't provide so much information that people are overwhelmed, but tell them how to get more details if they wish.

- Put appropriate information in appropriate places – your newsletter, forms that people complete and your website all need a different approach.

- Remember to ensure that you inform people whose data you get from someone else, unless it involves 'disproportionate effort'.

Examples

1) Vince runs a training programme. When organisations book people on to courses they obviously have to provide Personal Data about the participants. Vince thinks about what he does with the data and decides that he is confident that the Data Subjects know enough about what is going on. His organisation's name is prominent on the booking form, and he uses the information only for administering the training course and making sure everyone pays. The names of delegates are put on the computer, so they are Personal Data, but he decides not to put a Data Protection statement on the form.

However, the next time he runs a course he finds himself routinely printing off a list of participants and faxing it to the course tutor. He also normally puts a copy of the participants' list into the course packs. On reflection he decides that this may still be OK: he's only doing what people might expect; but he wants to be on the safe side. So he adds a short statement to his booking form explaining that the names and organisations, only, of the participants will be disclosed to the tutor in advance and to other participants.

The next development is that instead of marketing future courses to the participants' organisations, Vince decides to identify courses that people might be interested in and write directly to them. Because this is marketing directed to the individual, he now needs to make this clear on the form, and to offer an opt-out box.

He also decides that he needs to be more explicit when he collects information about special needs.

Vince ends up with a statement which says:

Information you provide in connection with our training courses will not be disclosed outside our organisation, except where necessary in order to facilitate the training. All participants are given a list of participants' names and organisations, but no further details.

If you do not want us to contact you in future about other training courses, events or publications, please tick this box [ ].

Information that you choose to give about your special needs will be passed to the venue and/or the tutor, if relevant, so that we can make your participation as rewarding as possible.

The Data Protection and confidentiality poster in an advice agency reads:

This agency has a strict policy on confidentiality and we take good care of any information we have about you. If you want to know more, please ask any of our advisers to explain or to give you a leaflet.

The clause at the bottom of a job application form could read:

All the information I have given here is true. I consent to the use of all this information for considering my application, and understand that:

- *it will be treated confidentially at all times;*
- *if I am successful it will form part of my personnel records;*
- *if I am unsuccessful the information will be destroyed after six months.*

Signed: _____ Date: _____

2) Manesh needs to carry out extensive equal opportunities monitoring of a youth training project. His manager suggests that the information collected could also be used to identify potential participants in special projects aimed at particular groups.

Manesh advises the manager that if they do this they cannot rely on the provisions for equalities monitoring, since they may end up using the information to make decisions about individuals. They therefore come up with the following statement for the form.

You do not have to provide any of this information, but if you do it will help us to make sure that you are getting the best help we can give you. We will not pass the information about you to anyone outside the project, but we will compile statistics to show our funders and other people how we are doing. This form will be kept separate from our other information about you and your progress, and will be destroyed once you leave the project.

Chapter 20

Working in collaboration with other organisations, statutory and voluntary

Working in collaboration with other organisations often raises complex Data Protection issues.

This chapter considers:

- The issues that arise when working in collaboration with other organisations
- The problems that may occur when voluntary organisations work alongside statutory bodies which have wider and different legal powers, and often a dominant role in the relationship

Who is the Data Controller?

The first requirement is always to identify the Data Controller. Possible relationships include the following examples.

- Each organisation is a separate Data Controller and the organisations merely disclose information to one other. In this case an information-sharing protocol may be useful.
- The organisations are joint Data Controllers. They share the same data, process it for the same purpose(s) and together make the decisions. A charity and a trading

company sharing the same marketing database, and using it to promote both the charity's fundraising and the trading company's products, for example, could be joint Data Controllers. Two or more organisations collaborating to run services for the same client group might be joint Data Controllers. Where there are joint Data Controllers, any one of them could be liable for any breach of the Act which occurs in relation to the shared set of data. In this case, a contract between the Data Controllers may well be advisable.

- The organisations are Data Controllers in common. They share some of the same data but for different purposes. Each Data Controller decides for itself the purposes it uses the data for, and is responsible for the parts of the data that relate only to its own purposes. This might apply, for example, if a school allowed a parents' association to use the names and addresses from its database of parents for regular fundraising contacts and to record the responses. The parents' association would have no access to or responsibility for the school-related part of the database, and the school would not have access to or responsibility for the fundraising section. In this case, an information-sharing protocol would probably be worth having.

- One organisation is the Data Controller with the other being a Data Processor. The Data Processor does not have the final say in the decisions about why or how the information is used (although it may provide professional advice or make recommendations because it has specific expertise to offer). In this case written evidence of the contract is required. This should normally be a binding agreement. In some cases an exchange of letters might be enough, but it is in the Data Controller's interests to protect itself contractually from any problems that might arise.

- The consortium itself is an independent Data Controller, disclosing information to and receiving information from its members. Where the consortium is a defined legal entity (such as a company set up for the purpose) this is quite likely. The situation becomes blurred when the consortium is run by a steering group or other body that is partially independent from its members. Legal advice may be required in such a situation.

Fair processing

If information being collected by one Data Controller will automatically be shared with one or more other Data Controllers, it is essential that the Data Subject is made aware of this when the information is obtained. If the sharing is not *necessary* for the purpose in mind, there is an argument that the Data Subject should be allowed to opt out. Certainly, if they do object, there is a danger of not complying with the Schedule 2 fair processing conditions: the Data Subject has not consented, so the first Condition is not met. It could be that the processing is necessary for a contract, or required by law, or falls under the definition of 'functions of a public nature' in Schedule 2(5)(d). But it could be that none of this applies. In that case you would have to argue that the processing was in the legitimate interests of the Data Controller(s) and that it did not prejudice the rights, freedoms or legitimate interests of the Data Subject; otherwise the processing could not take place.

It would also be good practice to ensure that the obligation to inform the Data Subject is recognised by all parties to the consortium. If possible, they should use a common statement or form of words. Only in that way can each of the collaborating organisations be confident that the requirement for transparency has been met and that their processing is fair.

Information-sharing protocols

When it is necessary to clarify in writing the conditions under which data will be shared and the respective Data Protection responsibilities each member of a consortium undertakes, an information-sharing protocol is often the best solution.[61]

A protocol should set out:

- who it applies to;
- general principles, including the basic principle of confidentiality and a recognition of the different requirements placed on different types of organisation (e.g. the Caldicott regime for NHS organisations);[62]
- the purposes for which information will be shared;
- procedures for sharing information, and in particular for getting and recording prior consent from the Data Subject, and defining the conditions in which disclosure may take place without consent;
- procedures to ensure that all parties have the same understanding of how to comply with all the Data Protection Principles – accuracy, retention periods, subject access, and so on;
- access and security procedures.

Working with statutory bodies

In certain respects, statutory bodies are subject to slightly different Data Protection requirements from voluntary organisations. These differences include the following points.

---

61 Government guidance on information-sharing protocols could, at the time of writing, be found on the old website of the Department for Constitutional Affairs (which was being retained as an archive) at www.foi.gov.uk/sharing/toolkit/infosharing.htm

62 Caldicott Guardians are responsible for overseeing good practice in respect of access to, and sharing of, confidential patient records. See www.connectingforhealth.nhs.uk/systemsandservices/infogov/caldicott/caldresources for a range of material to support Caldicott Guardians.

- The definition of data. 'Accessible records' are those relating to health, education, social work and housing to which access was previously granted under separate legislation. The 1998 Data Protection Act largely consolidated these with general Data Protection provisions, but there are a few remaining differences – for example Subject Access exists to the medical records of people after they have died, even though they are no longer Data Subjects.

- Manual data which has to be made available under the Freedom of Information Act 2000, even if it is not in a 'relevant filing system' (see Chapter 3).

- The fair processing conditions include the provision for 'functions of a public nature' not to require consent. While a statutory body is almost certain to be covered, voluntary organisations may well not be included.[63] Voluntary organisations are certainly not given special dispensation in Schedule 3, while many statutory bodies are able to process sensitive data without consent when carrying out their statutory functions.

- Statutory bodies can restrict Subject Access to health, education and social work records under certain conditions, while voluntary organisations do not have the same option.

- Statutory health and education providers can charge up to £50 for copies of material provided under Subject Access, in certain circumstances. Voluntary organisations are limited to the £10 maximum.

What this means is that where a voluntary and a statutory organisation share the same data, they have to be aware that Data Protection requirements may vary according to which Data Controller is under consideration. For example, a file could hypothetically contain some material that would be accessible under a Subject Access request to either Data Controller, some manual information not in a 'relevant filing system' which would only be accessible via the statutory body (under Freedom of Information), and some health or similar information that the statutory body could deny access to but the voluntary organisation could not.

Equally, there may be information that the statutory body can process without consent, but for which the voluntary organisation does need consent.

Wholesale sharing of information may not be in anyone's best interests. It may be better in many cases for each Data Controller to define which information they actually need, and then to restrict the transfer of information just to that information. Since each Data Controller is responsible for its own quality of data, it may even be better to make a referral with minimal data and then collect any other information required afresh from the Data Subject, if this can be done without unnecessary duplication of effort. Alternatively, an organisation could make the minimal referral, then get specific consent for transferring the remainder of the data.

---

63 See the discussion on page 45 concerning the Human Rights Act and the Freedom of Information Act, and the possibility of these being extended to cover voluntary organisations in some circumstances.

Summary

- Whenever two or more organisations work together, it is important to work out in advance who is, or who are, the Data Controller(s).

- Data Subjects must be made aware of any sharing of data that is likely to take place, and they must be given the chance to opt out if the sharing is not a necessary part of the service.

- It may be worth recording any agreements on sharing, confidentiality and security in an information-sharing protocol.

- Voluntary organisations should be aware that some Data Protection rules apply slightly differently to statutory bodies.

Example

Half a dozen projects in an inner city area get together to pool their services. Through a Lottery grant they are able to set up a client database to which they all have access. The idea is that anyone coming into contact with any of the participating organisations only has to go through one registration process. After that they can just turn up to use any of the services.

The steering committee for the project realises that there is a complex situation here. Can all the organisations be equally trusted to take good care of the client data? How will the clients feel about their information being shared? The committee decides that only a clear written policy will do, setting out:

- each organisation's responsibilities as a Data Controller;
- the security measures they will undertake;
- the protocols under which shared data can be used within each organisation.

In addition, the steering committee makes sure that the design of the database has strong security precautions built in – for example, so that people can normally see only the basic registration details of each client. If they need to see anything more sensitive they need authorisation, a good reason and a strictly controlled password.

Chapter 21

Notification

Most Data Controllers are required to 'notify' the Information Commissioner about their Data Processing activities. For them, it is a criminal offence not to do so.

This chapter looks at:

- How to work out whether you need to notify the Information Commissioner about your Data Processing activities
- The procedure involved in notification

One of the fundamental differences between the 1998 Data Protection Act and the old 1984 one concerns registration, now renamed notification. Under the 1984 Act, the very first question was 'Do we need to register?' If you did, the Act applied to you. If you didn't have to register, that was the end of the story and the Act did not apply.

All that has changed. The first question now is 'Are we a Data Controller?' If you are, all the preceding chapters of this book apply, and your responsibilities under the 1998 Act are considerable. A Data Controller may, in addition, have to 'notify' the Information Commissioner; on the other hand it may not, as there several exemptions from notification and it is possible to be completely exempt. The key point is that the Data Protection Principles and other provisions of the Act apply regardless. The question of notification is no longer central to everyone who is processing Personal Data.

However, for those who do have to notify, it does matter. Failing to notify when you should is a 'strict liability' criminal offence: you have no excuse if you get it wrong. 'I did my best' is not enough.

> **One of our management committee members was very hot on registration under the 1984 Act. Now that we have decided we do not have to notify under the 1998 Act, he is arguing that Data Protection is none of our concern. Is this right?**
>
> Emphatically not. If you are a Data Controller, then you must comply with the Act, whether or not you are also required to notify.

Do you need to notify?

You don't need to notify at all if all your processing of Personal Data is exempt. The Information Commissioner publishes a useful free booklet, *Notification exemptions: a self-assessment guide.*

If you are using the *Self-assessment guide*, you should note that you have to take the questions in order. If you get as far as Question 4 (which lists activities that must be notified) and answer 'yes', then you must notify. Only if you can answer 'no' do you carry on, eventually, to Question 8 where the exemption for non-profit organisations is covered.

The exemptions fall into two main categories.

- Manually held data is completely exempt from notification under the terms of the Act itself. If you notify a system that is partly held manually and partly on computer, you have to indicate just that there is additional manual material.
- Certain 'core business purposes' have been exempted from notification by Regulation,[64] even if the data is held on computer.

The core business purposes are:

- personnel administration, including payroll, and including volunteers;
- accounts and customer/supplier records;
- marketing, promotion and public relations for your own organisation (which might, for example, cover a mailing list used to send out annual reports and other general promotional material);
- membership records of non-profit organisations.

In each case there are limitations. Generally the Data Subjects, the types of data held and any disclosures must be restricted to those 'necessary' for the purpose, in order to claim the exemption.

---

64 Statutory Instrument 2000 No. 188.

You may voluntarily notify activities that are exempt. If you are not sure whether to notify, it is often easier to notify anyway, and the cost (£35 a year at the time of writing) is not significant.

Who has to notify?

Notification must be made by the Data Controller. Remember that you cannot be a Data Controller on someone else's behalf. Therefore, each Data Controller has to consider separately whether notification is required. A charity may be exempt while its associated trading company has to notify, for example. A national organisation might need to notify while some of its local branches are exempt, but others, perhaps because they keep information on computer rather than manually, also have to notify on their own account.

Notification procedure

Notification can be initiated in three ways:

- on the Internet – through the Information Commissioner's website;
- by phone, to the Information Commissioner – at the time of writing the number is 01625 545740;
- by obtaining a notification form from the Information Commissioner.

In each case you first have to provide details of the Data Controller. Guidance is available from the Information Commissioner on how to complete these details. For example, in the case of a limited company you have to provide the full company name, not a trading name. An individual has to provide their full name.

In an attempt to simplify the notification process, once you have indicated the general nature of your activities the Information Commissioner can generate a draft notification based on 'typical' activities for that type of business. This will be sent to you (if you phoned up), or can be printed off (if you used the Internet). You make any corrections necessary, sign it and send it off with the fee.

The bulk of the notification is concerned with the purposes for which you process data. You are offered a list of standard purposes to choose from (see the box on pages 152–3). For each Purpose that applies to you, you then have to specify your Data Subjects, Data Classes, potential recipients of data and any overseas transfers of Personal Data.

If the draft you receive from the Information Commissioner does not accurately reflect what you do, you can add or delete purposes and, within each purpose, Data Subjects, Data Classes, recipients and overseas transfers. In each case you can make up your own entry if the standard ones don't apply. You cannot normally use a purpose twice.

One feature from the 1984 registration scheme which is missing from notification is the need to indicate your sources of information. In addition the standard lists of potential Data Subjects, Data Classes and recipients are significantly shorter. This makes completion of the forms both quicker and more accurate than it used to be.

In the final part of the notification you have to describe in general terms your security measures (see Chapter 14 for more on this), together with various other pieces of additional information.

Notification costs £35 per year for each Data Controller, regardless of how many purposes you have. This means that if any of your purposes have to be notified it costs nothing for you voluntarily to add any other purposes for which you process Personal Data, even if they are exempt. No Data Controller can normally have more than one notification.

If you have decided that you and one or more other organisations are joint Data Controllers for a particular activity, it may be worth coordinating your notification efforts to ensure consistency.

Where services are provided to a standard national pattern by a number of independent local groups in a federation, it may be worth the federation producing a model notification entry and seeking the Information Commissioner's endorsement. If this is done, it must still be made clear that any local group cannot just use the model without checking that it really does reflect their activities.

After notification

Once your notification has been accepted it remains valid for one year. Near the end of that time the Information Commissioner will remind you to renew it.

You have to keep your notification up to date. If any of the details change, either about the Data Controller or about your activities, you have to ensure that an amendment form is submitted within 28 days. There is no charge for this. Failure to do it is a criminal offence.

You cannot transfer your notification. This means that if you change your legal status (for example, by becoming a limited company or amalgamating with another organisation) the new organisation has to notify from scratch in its own right.

Standard notification purposes

Staff administration
Advertising, marketing and public relations
Accounts and records
Accounting and auditing (for other people)
Administration of justice

Administration of membership records
Advertising, marketing and public relations for others
Assessment and collection of taxes and other revenue
Benefits, grants and loans administration
Canvassing political support among the electorate
Constituency casework
Consultancy and advisory services
Credit referencing
Crime prevention and prosecution of offenders
Debt administration and factoring
Education
Fundraising
Health administration and services
Information and databank administration
Insurance administration
Journalism and media
Legal services
Licensing and registration
Pastoral care
Pensions administration
Policing
Private investigation
Processing for not-for-profit organisations (membership and related services)
Property management
Provision of financial services and advice
Realising the objectives of a charitable organisation or voluntary body
Research
Trading/sharing in personal information

In nearly all cases the Information Commissioner's guidance goes on to expand on what each of these purposes is expected to cover.

Standard notification Data Subjects

S100 Staff, including volunteers, agents, temporary and casual workers
S101 Customers and clients
S102 Suppliers
S103 Members or supporters
S104 Complainants, correspondents and enquirers
S105 Relatives, guardians and associates of the Data Subject
S106 Advisers, consultants and other professional experts
S107 Patients
S108 Students and pupils
S109 Offenders and suspected offenders

Standard notification Data Classes

C200 Personal details
C201 Family, lifestyle and social circumstances
C202 Education and training details
C203 Employment details
C204 Financial details
C205 Goods or services provided
C206 Racial or ethnic origin
C207 Political opinions
C208 Religious or other beliefs of a similar nature
C209 Trade union membership
C210 Physical or mental health or condition
C211 Sexual life
C212 Offences (including alleged offences)
C213 Criminal proceedings, outcomes and sentences

Summary

- Any Data Controller may, potentially, have to notify the Information Commissioner about their Data Protection activities.

- Notification can be initiated by telephone or on the notification website, where further guidance is available, or by requesting an application form.

- The annual fee is £35 (at the time of writing), regardless of the size or complexity of the activities being notified.

- Certain activities (including all manual processing) are exempt from notification. However, this does not exempt them from any other aspect of the Act.

- Exempt activities may be notified voluntarily.

- Failure to notify when it is required is a criminal offence.

Chapter 22

Enforcement, offences and penalties

The Act gives the Information Commissioner important enforcement powers. The Commissioner has argued that these are insufficient, and should be strengthened.

This chapter summarises:

- The powers of the Information Commissioner
- The penalties for breach of the Act

The Data Protection Act is enforced by the Information Commissioner, who also has responsibility for the Privacy and Electronic Communications (EC Directive) Regulations 2003 and (in England and Wales) for enforcing Freedom of Information. The Commissioner's Office is an independent regulatory authority, reporting directly to Parliament.

The first Data Protection Registrar, from 1985, was Eric Howe. His successor was Elizabeth France, who briefly became Data Protection Commissioner under the 1998 Act, then Information Commissioner when Freedom of Information was added to her responsibilities. When her term of office finished in November 2002, Richard Thomas took over the post.

The Commissioner does not have a large staff – around 250 at the time of writing. Data Protection activities are funded solely by income from notification fees and other charges – amounting to nearly £11 million in 2007–08. Freedom of Information activities are funded by government grant – just over £5 million in 2007–08.

The 1998 Act for the first time gave the Information Commissioner's staff powers of entry and inspection when they are investigating breaches of the Act.

Codes of practice

An important provision in the 1998 Act is that the Information Commissioner now has both a power and a duty to promote good practice. In particular, he can endorse Codes of Practice for particular types of activity or industry sectors. If he believes a Code of Practice is necessary and the industry has not produced one, he can even impose one of his own.

Failure to adhere to a Code of Practice could be viewed adversely by the courts. Codes must, therefore, be legally watertight and the process of producing them is lengthy. At the time of writing the Commissioner had issued only two Codes (both revised since their initial publication): one on closed circuit television (CCTV) and one on employment records.

Given the time and effort that it takes to produce formal Codes of Practice, these appear likely to remain few and far between. What the Commissioner has been doing, however, is to produce guidance notes on a wide range of subjects, generally those on which he has concerns, or where the number of enquiries is large. When faced with a Data Protection problem it is always worth visiting the Commissioner's website and looking in the document library to see whether any relevant guidance exists.

Notification

Notification is one aspect of enforcement. Processing without having notified when you should have done so is an offence. This is a 'strict liability' offence: you cannot argue that you did your best. It is also an offence not to keep your notification up to date. On this you *can* argue that you exercised 'due diligence'.

The Information Commissioner has a policy of encouraging Data Controllers to notify, rather than taking immediate enforcement action. There have, however, been a series of prosecutions where Data Controllers have ignored the Information Commissioner's reminders. For example, in March 2005 a solicitor was fined £3,150 plus £3,500 costs for failing to notify, after five reminders from the Information Commissioner. Two debt collection agencies were similarly fined £5,000 each plus £300 costs, in October 2005, after three and five reminders. Generally, however, the penalties for failing to notify have been around £300 plus a similar amount in costs.

Assessments

Anyone may ask the Information Commissioner to make an Assessment as to whether a Data Controller appears to be complying with the Act. The person making the request must believe themselves to be directly affected by the processing they want assessed. The Commissioner *must* then make an Assessment, provided he has enough information to identify the person making the request and the processing in question.

The Commissioner can choose how to make the Assessment. He can specifically take into account:

- whether the request raises a matter of substance;
- any undue delay in making the request;
- whether the person is entitled to make a Subject Access request.

What this appears to mean is that requests for Assessment should not be used when the matter could have been resolved directly with the Data Controller or through a Subject Access request. If the Commissioner thinks this is the case, it may affect how the Assessment is carried out.

The Commissioner has to tell the person making the request whether he has made an Assessment, and may – but is not obliged to – tell them the outcome.

An Assessment is only the Commissioner's opinion, but would obviously carry some weight if the matter later came to court.

A complaint form, asking the Commissioner to make an Assessment, is available from the Information Commissioner's Office.

Information notices

The Commissioner may issue a Data Controller with an Information Notice, either as part of an Assessment or for reasons of his own. This will ask the Data Controller to provide specific information within a specified time limit, with the aim of enabling the Commissioner to decide whether the Data Protection Principles are being complied with.

Failure to comply with an Information Notice is an offence, unless the Data Controller can show that they 'exercised due diligence' to comply. The Data Controller can appeal against an Information Notice to the Information Tribunal.

Enforcement notices

Where the Commissioner is satisfied that the Act has been contravened he can issue an Enforcement Notice, telling the Data Controller what they must do in order to bring their activities into line.

Failure to comply with an Enforcement Notice is an offence, unless the Data Controller can show that they 'exercised due diligence' to comply. The Data Controller can appeal against an Enforcement Notice to the Information Tribunal.

Powers of entry

The Commissioner can apply for a warrant from a circuit judge to enter and inspect premises if he has reasonable grounds for suspecting that an offence under the Act has been committed or that the Data Protection Principles are being broken.

The warrant may be granted only if the Information Commissioner has tried to get access by agreement and been refused, unless the judge is convinced that giving advance warning would defeat the object.

It is a criminal offence to obstruct a warrant, with a maximum fine of £5,000.

Individual offences

In addition to the offence of obstructing a warrant, individuals commit an offence if they 'knowingly or recklessly' obtain or disclose Personal Data without authorisation from the Data Controller. Possible defences include having the 'reasonable belief' that what they did was permissible.

If a person has obtained data they are not entitled to, it is a further offence to sell it or offer to sell it.

It may be worth making staff, volunteers and trustees/management committee members who have access to Personal Data aware of these provisions.

In the light of a series of serious security breaches towards the end of 2007, the case has been put forward that these should attract criminal penalties (for the individual responsible and/or the Data Controller), rather than just being treated as breaches of the Principles.

Penalties

All offences under the Act, except obstructing a warrant, can be tried either in the Magistrate's Court or the Crown Court. The maximum penalty is a fine of £5,000 in the Magistrate's Court or an unlimited fine in the Crown Court.

The Commissioner has argued that imprisonment should be an option in the worst cases of deliberate theft of Personal Data, and this was under consideration at the time of writing.

Who gets taken to court, should it come to that, depends on the offence. Where the offence is an individual one, it is obviously the individual who would be charged. Where the organisation has committed an offence to do with notification or not cooperating with the Commissioner, the organisation would be charged. However, an unincorporated association (see Appendix A) cannot be taken to court in its own right. In this case it would most likely be one or more of the members of the board or management committee who would end up being personally charged.

If your organisation is incorporated, the directors or senior officers may also be personally liable if they consented to or connived at the offence, or if they were negligent.

The Information Commissioner also received powers[65] in May 2008 to levy a financial penalty on a Data Controller, where the Commissioner is satisfied that they have seriously breached the Principles. At the time of writing, there was no indication what level of penalty might be imposed, but it is worth pointing out, for example, that the Financial Services Authority (FSA), in one case, levied a penalty of £900,000 for the loss of customer data by the Nationwide Building Society.[66]

Compensation and redress

The Information Commissioner cannot award compensation or force a Data Controller to put matters right directly. (The Commissioner would have to issue an Enforcement Notice, then take the Data Controller to court if they did not comply.) An individual seeking compensation or other forms of redress has to take a civil case against the Data Controller (see page 73).

Summary

The 1998 Data Protection Act is enforced by the Information Commissioner. The Commissioner can:

- produce, endorse and promote Codes of Practice;
- make an Assessment;
- issue an Information Notice;
- issue an Enforcement Notice;
- apply for a warrant to enter and inspect premises.

Failure to notify and failure to keep a notification up to date are offences.

Individuals commit an offence if they knowingly or recklessly get access to data without permission or permit someone else to have unauthorised access, and a second offence if they then try to sell it.

The maximum penalty for any offence is £5,000 if tried in the Magistrate's Court, but most can also be tried in the Crown Court, with unlimited fines. Custodial sentences for deliberate theft of Personal Data are under consideration.

---

65 The Criminal Justice and Immigration Act 2008 introduced a substantial amendment to the Data Protection Act setting out these powers. For the full text of the Data Protection Act with all current amendments (and indeed for all other current legislation), see www.statutelaw.gov.uk
66 The FSA can penalise the businesses it regulates for any material breach of the law. In this case, it was a Data Protection Act breach.

Chapter 23

Taking stock: Data Protection audits and policy development

There are so many strands to Data Protection that it is often difficult to know where to begin. For many organisations, the first step is to identify gaps in their systems and then take action to fill them.

This chapter:

- Describes an approach based on the Information Commissioner's recommendations on Data Protection auditing
- Looks at how to draw up appropriate policies
- Offers advice on where guidance may be found, including the Commissioner's Codes of Practice

The first thing you may need to do is to assess where you are with Data Protection: what activities are covered, how good your existing policies and procedure are, and so on. This is sometimes called a Data Protection audit.

The Information Commissioner has produced guidance on carrying out such an audit. The Commissioner's scheme is exhaustive, and probably too elaborate for many small voluntary organisations. However, the general approach has much to recommend it. The process is split into two parts: an 'adequacy' audit and a 'compliance' audit. In essence, the adequacy audit asks: 'Has the organisation identified its processing of Personal Data, made the necessary decisions and produced the necessary policies?' The compliance audit then looks at whether the policies are being followed and the Data Protection Principles complied with.

As with any audit, it is possible to carry out the procedure internally, using your own staff, or externally, for greater objectivity (but, inevitably, at much greater cost). Your choice on whether to buy in support may partly depend on whether you have the necessary expertise in house. The Commissioner recommends that the adequacy part of the audit is best done externally.

The adequacy audit

An adequacy audit is largely a desk exercise. It is supposed to check that existing policies comply with Data Protection requirements. Inevitably, however, many organisations will already be aware that they have work to do in some areas. If you are in this situation, it may be a more economical use of time to combine the auditing process with the remedy: where policies do not exist, they can be drawn up, using the impetus of the audit.

The audit may also throw up specific tasks that need to be undertaken: many organisations find that they need to work out who all their Data Processors are and systematically review their contracts.

In other cases legal advice may be required to answer apparently simple questions, such as 'who is the Data Controller?', before you can decide who is responsible for drawing up policies.

Finally, the audit should identify lines of accountability and responsibility within the organisation, from the board of trustees or management committee to those staff or volunteers who actually handle the Personal Data.

Identifying relevant policies is not always easy. Typically, they will be scattered in a number of places, such as staff handbooks, confidentiality policies or fundraising guidelines. It is often useful to start by thinking about key types of Data Subject (clients, personnel, and so on) or different situations (marketing or case recording, for example), and then ask the relevant staff and volunteers what written policies they have produced or are aware of in those areas.

Almost inevitably you will realise that the policies you find do not cover all aspects of Data Protection, and may even be inconsistent with each other. It will probably be necessary to draft additional material or amend existing documents, and to prepare a summary showing how all the different documents relate to each other.

Subsequently, adequacy audits should be much more straightforward, as they will be able to review a complete set of documentation.

Policies

Many organisations would like to shorten the process by starting from model Data Protection policies. But good Data Protection practice is based on the Data Protection

Principles, not rules, and the Principles have to be applied according to the particular circumstances of each organisation. Because of this, it is hard to offer examples without making them so general that you may as well start from scratch. In addition, a policy on its own is not enough to guarantee good Data Protection practice. Your staff, and others who handle Personal Data on your behalf, have to know what your policy is and how to apply it. It is these day-to-day procedures – which may or may not need to be written down, but which must be consistent throughout your organisation – that make all the difference (see following chapter).

What may help, however, is to consider what type of policy framework will best fit your organisation. There are at least three possible approaches.

- A comprehensive Data Protection policy that covers all the issues in one document.

- An overview Data Protection policy with most of the detail in a set of separate functional policies (confidentiality, case recording, marketing, and so on).

- An overview Data Protection policy with most of the detail in a set of policies divided by types of Data Subject (members, staff, volunteers, clients, and so on).

The advantage of a single policy is that all your Data Protection material is in one place. There are, however, several disadvantages. One is that the policy may be quite large, and people working in specific areas of your organisation may have to wade through a lot of material that is not relevant to them. This means that they will be less likely to make themselves aware of the bits that do apply to them. Another is that it may be difficult to draw clear boundaries. If you are dealing with confidentiality in the Data Protection policy, for example, what do you do about the aspects of confidentiality that are not strictly related to Data Protection?

A template for a comprehensive Data Protection policy has been produced by Lasa, and is available on its website.[67]

Incorporating Data Protection issues into other policies may make for more manageable and coherent documents – but it is probably more work keeping a whole set of policies up to date and consistent. The choice between a functional focus and a Data Subject focus depends on the audience for the policies: if they are mainly to guide staff, then a functional approach may be better; if they are mainly to inform Data Subjects, then ones that are based around Data Subjects might be more suitable.

In either case you will also need an overall policy which covers those aspects of Data Protection that do not sit easily with anything else, and which allocates responsibilities. An example of an overall Data Protection policy is given opposite, but note that this is just an example. It should only be used to help you in developing your own policy, not as a model.

---

67 Lasa is the London Advice Services Alliance, and the template can be found (at the time of writing) at: www.ictknowledgebase.org.uk/dataprotectionpolicies. The main Lasa website is at: www.lasa.org.uk

Example Data Protection policy

Introduction and general principles

Our organisation is committed to good practice in the handling of Personal Data and careful compliance with the requirements of the Data Protection Act.

Our first priority is to avoid causing harm to individuals. In the main this means:

- keeping information securely in the right hands;
- holding good-quality information.

Second, we will ensure that the legitimate concerns of individuals about the ways in which their data may be used are taken into account. In particular, we will aim to be open and transparent in the way we use Personal Data, and will seek to give individuals as much choice as is possible and reasonable over what data is held and how it is used.

Operational procedures and guidance to staff will set out more detailed ways in which these objectives can be achieved.

Responsibilities

The board of our organisation recognises its overall legal responsibility for Data Protection compliance.

Day-to-day responsibility for Data Protection is delegated to a nominated Data Protection Officer, currently the Finance Director. The main responsibilities of the Data Protection Officer are:

- briefing the board on Data Protection responsibilities as required;
- reviewing Data Protection and related policies at appropriate intervals;
- advising other staff on tricky Data Protection issues;
- ensuring that Data Protection induction and training takes place;
- keeping our notification with the Information Commissioner up to date;
- handling any Subject Access requests;
- approving unusual or controversial disclosures of Personal Data;
- approving contracts with Data Processors.

All managers of departments, teams and functional areas have the following responsibilities.

- Assisting the Data Protection Officer in identifying aspects of their area of work that have Data Protection implications so that guidance can be provided as necessary.
- Ensuring that their operational procedures take full account of Data Protection requirements.
- Including Data Protection and confidentiality in staff induction and training (for temporary staff and volunteers as well as permanent staff).

All staff are responsible for understanding and complying with the procedures that we have adopted in order to ensure Data Protection compliance.

Storage of Personal Data in electronic form

To assist with Data Protection compliance (and in particular the requirements that data be accurate and be held securely) all staff are required to use the central contact database as their primary store for data about individuals they are in contact with in any way. If the central database does not meet the needs of any particular activity, the IT Manager must first be consulted about whether it can be modified to meet these needs.

Only if this is not possible may a separate data set be constructed, in which case the IT Manager and the Data Protection Officer must be informed.

Specific legal provisions

We will not make a charge for Subject Access. [or . . . will not make a charge for Subject Access by current staff or members or anyone who has attended an event within the previous year, but will charge £10 for all other Subject Access requests.]

We will make a voluntary Notification to the Information Commissioner, even if all our data-processing activities are potentially exempt from Notification.

All contracts between our organisation and Data Processors will be reviewed by the Data Protection Officer for compliance with Data Protection Act requirements.

Related policies

This policy should be read alongside the following policies and procedures which cover specific aspects of our Data Protection responsibilities.

- Confidentiality and privacy policy.
- Security policy.
- Case recording guidelines.
- Agreed statements to be used throughout our organisation when offering marketing and fundraising opt-ins and opt-outs.

When drawing up other policies, a checklist for possible Data Protection issues might be useful. The key points are likely to include the following questions.

- Are all the individuals about whom data is collected likely to be aware of the uses that we make of information about them, and in particular to whom it may be disclosed? If not, there should be a procedure to inform them (usually at the point where information is first obtained).

- Have all individuals been given the opportunity to opt out of receiving marketing material, where applicable?

- Where we intend marketing by phone or e-mail, have all individuals been asked for their consent to being approached in this way?

- Where we intend sharing personal details with other organisations, have all individuals been given the opportunity to opt out?
- Are mailing and other contact preferences reliably recorded on the central database (or other appropriate place)?
- When mailings and other marketing contacts take place are individuals' preferences fully respected?
- Are all booking forms and other data collection documents compliant with the guidance on fair processing statements?
- Can all the data held about individuals be justified (as adequate, relevant and not excessive), and are there procedures to ensure its accuracy?
- Is there a clear understanding of the time after which data which has not been checked for accuracy will be deemed too unreliable for continued use?
- Is there a clear retention period for all data?
- Are all staff who handle data aware of the extent to which it is confidential?
- Are there adequate security measures to protect the data, especially when it leaves the main office for any reason (working at home or at an event, for example)?
- If any Personal Data is to be transferred abroad (even under the exclusive control of our staff) has the Data Protection Officer been consulted about any precautions or specific arrangements which may need to be made?

If you are preparing policies relating to specific types of Data Subject it may also be worth narrowing down the issues which are likely to be important. For example, with clients, the main issue might be confidentiality and disclosures (for example, disclosures you have to make to other agencies or funders). For donors, the issue may centre on the marketing opt-out. Staff may be most concerned with Subject Access, especially for specific parts of their record, such as references.

If possible your policies should represent your existing practice, unless you find that key decisions have not been made, or that your practice is not compliant with Data Protection. In this case you will not only have to write the policy appropriately, but also ensure that the change in practice is effectively communicated to all your staff (after approval by your board of trustees, if necessary).

Do not be tempted to write too much. A short, clear policy is likely to be far more effective than a detailed one that no one uses. Rather than going into detail about every possible eventuality, your policies should normally cover just the things that are likely to happen routinely. Line managers and your Data Protection Officer should then be available to deal with anything out of the ordinary.

Example[68]

An agency has the following statement prominently displayed in its waiting room:

Nothing you tell us leaves the agency without your consent except in rare instances. If you would like to know more about what happens to the information we collect, please ask for a leaflet.

The leaflet is made up of two sides of A5. One side says:

You will already be aware that while you have been talking to someone here, that person has been writing down some notes about you.

It is important to let you know how we use that information and how we ensure that it cannot be misused in any way.

We will not normally use your data in a way you would not wish. This includes keeping any information you give us about yourself confidential at all times except in very specific circumstances (see the reverse side of this page).

The reason we take information about you, in the first instance, is so that the person you are seeing can read back over this information and think how best to support you, which may involve sharing some information with appropriate colleagues. You can take a copy of this information away with you if you wish.

The other reason we keep your information is for statistical purposes, so that we can make sure we are providing the right kind of service for as many people as possible. We also give some of the statistical data to the people who fund us, but we must make it clear that no one can be identified through this data (for example, we tell our funders how many males and females have contacted us – obviously completely anonymously).

If you have any specific questions about how we use your information or look after it, please ask any of our staff.

Additionally, if you have any suggestions for us on how we can give you a better service, please let us know.

The other side of the leaflet says:

Confidentiality

Any information that you give about yourself when you are here is confidential to the agency and will not be given out to anyone without your express permission.

You should be aware that there are four occasions when we have no choice about what remains confidential. They are:

---

68 This example is used with permission. It has been slightly edited to avoid identifying the source.

- if there is a real concern that you are putting a third person at risk, e.g. suspected child abuse;
- where we are instructed to do so by the social services department under specific legislation;
- when we are required to do so under the Prevention of Terrorism Act 1989, the Drug Trafficking Offences Act 1986, other legislation requiring disclosure or during an investigation by the Serious Fraud Squad;
- should you fall seriously ill while you are here and we have to give information to medical personnel.

The compliance audit

Once you have a policy or set of policies, there is something to measure your Data Protection performance against. To do this thoroughly can be time consuming; again it is worth setting priorities so that you devote your energy to the issues likely to be threats, either to your own activities or to the interests of your Data Subjects. You may find that some areas of your policy are almost self-policing; with personnel records, for example, it is quite likely that any major problems would come to your attention by other means. A 'light touch' compliance audit may just consist of an annual interview with the Personnel Officer to go over their procedures and perhaps a questionnaire to staff and volunteers from time to time to allow them to raise any concerns.

With clients or members, however, you are likely to have to be more formal and systematic. You should:

- examine all the relevant documents, including forms, brochures, standard letters, web pages and so on, to ensure that your statements are clear, accurate and consistent, and that relevant opt-outs are offered;
- go through any written procedures to check that they pay due attention to Data Protection;
- look at the recording system to make sure it is structured so as to hold the relevant information;
- review a sample of records (paying due attention to confidentiality) to spot any possible problems with data quality, retention periods and so on;
- interview relevant staff to check that their daily practice is based on an understanding of the policy and any written procedures.

Guidance on good practice

As time goes on, guidance on procedures and good practice is emerging. The Information Commissioner's website holds a growing list of documents addressing numerous specific issues, while many national organisations, umbrella bodies and professional associations have also produced practical guidance in their areas of interest.

As previously mentioned, the Information Commissioner has produced Codes of Practice in two areas. These are not definitive statements on the law. However, they do carry legal weight as official recommendations as to how the legal requirements can be met. If you do not follow a Code, you must be able to show how your alternative solution complies with the Act, and you may have to justify your approach if the Commissioner takes enforcement action.

At the time of writing, a consultation exercise on a revised Code on Closed Circuit Television (CCTV) systems had been carried out, but the Code itself was still in draft form. A summary for small users was also available, which says that:

- cameras should be sited so that their images are clear enough to allow the police to use them to investigate a crime;
- cameras should be positioned to avoid capturing the images of people not visiting the premises;
- there should be signs so that people visiting the premises know a CCTV system is in operation, and the Data Controller's contact details should be on the sign if it is not obvious who is responsible for the system;
- the recorded images from the CCTV system should be securely stored, where only a limited number of authorised persons may have access to them;
- the recorded images should only be retained long enough for any incident to come to light (e.g. for a theft to be noticed);
- recordings should only be made available to law enforcement agencies involved in the prevention and detection of crime, and no other third parties;
- the operating equipment should be regularly checked to ensure that it is working properly (e.g. the recording media is good enough and features such as the date and time stamp are correctly set).

Of more interest to most voluntary organisations is likely to be the Code of Practice on employment records. This was much delayed. It emerged in four sections, each of which repeated much of the general material. It was then reissued as a single, and slightly simplified, document. The Code is lengthy and detailed, but it is worth looking at its recommendations. Again, there is a summary version, intended for small businesses, and appropriate for many voluntary organisations. After an introduction, separate sections cover the following points.

- Recruitment and selection.
- Employment records.
- Monitoring at work.
- Information about workers' health.
- Workers' rights.

See also the Directory of Social Change *Employment Records Handbook* (see Further information) for a more detailed treatment of this topic.

Summary

- An 'adequacy audit' involves checking that you have the right policies in place.
- A 'compliance audit' involves checking that these policies are complied with.
- These audits can be carried out by your own staff, but a small amount of external input is often advisable.
- Although you will want to avoid unnecessary paperwork, key policies and decisions must be documented.
- Where the Information Commissioner has produced a Code of Practice, it is advisable to be aware of its provisions and to follow them where applicable.

Chapter 24

Training your staff and encouraging good Data Protection practice

This topic deserves a chapter of its own, because it is the key to Data Protection compliance. You can understand the Act, draw up policies and design systems that guide people towards compliance, but if your staff and volunteers don't understand what to do, and how to do it effectively, none of this effort will have the desired effect.

This chapter:

- Suggests a training strategy and includes a suggested basic briefing on the Act
- Looks at where Data Protection responsibility might be located within your organisation

Staff and volunteers are your biggest security risk where Data Protection is concerned. Problems can, of course, arise from external intrusion or from deliberate unauthorised access. But far more often, it is people who are authorised to have access, but are then careless or unwitting in the way they use the information, who cause trouble.

The key to effective training in this area is 'little and often'. By reminding people regularly of their responsibilities, not only do you keep them alert, you also build Data Protection into the culture of your organisation. Instead of issuing memos and lengthy written guidance, or relying on people's induction training – when Data Protection will be one of hundreds of topics they have to absorb – it is probably more effective to spend 15 minutes at a quarterly staff meeting giving your team a case study and discussing the correct course of action.

Your training programme may look something like this.

- A briefing for your board of trustees or management committee and senior management team, outlining their main responsibilities. This may need to be repeated every two or three years.

- Training for a small number of staff – or just one, depending on the size of your organisation – who will have Data Protection responsibilities in their job description. They will then be able to work on any audits, policies or procedures you need.

- Incorporation of basic Data Protection into your induction programme for new staff and volunteers, especially covering confidentiality and security.

- Initial basic Data Protection training for all your existing staff and volunteers.

- Preparation of simple reminders that people can refer to in specific, rare situations – for example what to do if a Data Subject makes a Subject Access request, what to do if the police or another official agency asks for information.

- Regular inclusion of case studies and snippets of Data Protection good practice in team meetings.

You should encourage staff to consider the Data Protection aspects of all new projects and activities. For example, there are bound to be implications if you embark on a new collaborative activity, if you set up a website, or if you outsource a piece of work to a new Data Processor. It should be one of the items that must be checked off before authorisation is given to go ahead.

When you carry out staff monitoring, supervision and appraisal, you should pay attention to any Data Protection responsibilities the person has.

Briefing documents

One of the difficulties with Data Protection is that it is hard to understand individual elements in isolation. You often need the whole picture, or certainly a large part of it. The following sample briefing sheet is not intended to answer all the questions, but to provide a context in which you can go on to point out in more detail the specific implications for your organisation. You may wish to use something like this (with local adaptations) in briefing your management committee or board and those staff and volunteers who just need the minimum introduction to the Act.

Briefing on Data Protection

The underlying purposes of Data Protection are:

- To prevent harm to individuals by:
  - keeping data only in the right hands;
  - holding good quality data (accurate, up to date and adequate).

- To allay people's concerns about how their data might be used, and to demonstrate respect for their interests by:
  - making sure people know enough about what you are doing with their data – not keeping them in the dark or going behind their backs;
  - giving people a choice where this is reasonable and possible.

When you HOLD Personal Data

- You are allowed to use it only for the purpose(s) for which it was originally obtained.
- You have to take good care of it. (Security must be 'appropriate'.)
- You have to use it 'fairly'.
- You must ensure that it is: adequate, relevant, not excessive, accurate, up to date if necessary, and not held longer than necessary.

When you OBTAIN Personal Data

- You have be transparent. This means making sure that the person from whom you are getting the data knows which organisation is collecting the data, and why and how the data will be used.
- You must not deceive or mislead anyone.
- If you get the data from someone other than the individual themselves (the 'Data Subject'), you have to make sure that the Data Subject knows as soon as practicable who is using their data and why and how it will be used.
- You may have to get consent from the Data Subject to use their data, particularly if it is in any of the 'sensitive' categories. ('Sensitive' data covers the Data Subject's racial or ethnic origin, religious or political beliefs, trade union membership, health, sex life or criminal record.)
- You may also have to offer them the chance to opt out of some uses of the data, such as direct marketing, disclosure to other organisations, or use for secondary purposes.

When you DISCLOSE Personal Data

- You have to check that the disclosure fits the purpose or purposes for which the data is being held.
- You have to check that the person you are disclosing it to is authorised to have it.
- You have to check that the Data Subject is aware that this type of disclosure is possible, and either that the disclosure will not cause any harm to the individual or infringe their rights, or that there is an overriding reason for disclosure (such as a legal obligation).

- If you put Personal Data on to the web, you may need consent from the Data Subject.
- If you transfer data outside the European Economic Area (EU plus Iceland, Liechtenstein and Norway) special rules might apply.

Data Subjects have new RIGHTS

- Where you need a person's consent, you can't use the data if they don't give consent (but you can explain the consequences of not giving it).
- You cannot use data for direct marketing of any goods or services if the Data Subject has told you not to.
- If you are phoning people at home for direct marketing, you have to check that the number you are calling is not on the Telephone Preference Service register, and there are restrictions on marketing by fax or e-mail.
- Data Subjects can ask to see virtually all the Personal Data you hold on them, including manual files. The organisation has 40 days to comply with the request and can charge up to £10.

Legal responsibility

- Responsibility for complying with Data Protection lies with the 'Data Controller' – normally the organisation, rather than individual paid staff or volunteers.
- Individuals commit an offence if they 'knowingly or recklessly' access or use data without authorisation.

Allocating responsibility

Although your board or management committee has ultimate responsibility and Data Protection must also be a concern of the senior management team, most organisations find that they need to identify a member of staff who takes a lead on Data Protection on a day-to-day basis. In small organisations there may be little choice as to who takes on this role. Larger organisations, however, often find it hard to work out the best place to locate their Data Protection compliance role.

Options include:

- **The chief officer, or their deputy**

  Because Data Protection can affect virtually any part of the organisation, this may be the only suitable solution.

- **The company secretary**

  This may be appropriate if your main emphasis is on Data Protection as a compliance issue.

- **The legal department**

  This has the benefit of putting Data Protection on the same footing as a range of other legal matters, but it may be somewhat remote from day-to-day operations.

- **Internal audit or quality standards**

  The advantage of putting Data Protection here is that the activities giving rise to the most serious Data Protection concerns are likely to be covered.

- **Information services**

  Because there are substantial elements of information management in Data Protection, it may be appropriate to use people with these specific skills as a central resource for the organisation.

- **Fundraising or public relations**

  Good Data Protection practice can enhance an organisation's image and help to build trust with those outside.

- **Trading or customer services**

  For some organisations most Data Protection issues are likely to arise between the organisation and customers or service users, especially over marketing opt-outs.

- **Human resources**

  If an organisation has relatively little contact with individuals outside, most of the Data Protection questions that arise may be to do with staff records.

- **Information technology**

  In the past it was common to make the IT Manager responsible for Data Protection, because it applied only to data held on computer. Now that Data Protection extends to manual records, this is less appropriate. The IT department does still need to be involved, however.

For an example of how the responsibilities of such a Data Protection Officer could be set out, see the sample Data Protection policy in the previous chapter.

Summary

- You must brief your board of trustees or management committee on its responsibilities.
- Training your paid staff and volunteers is more important for Data Protection compliance than large amounts of paperwork.
- Initial induction training should be topped up regularly with brief reminders.
- Guidance notes should be short and to the point.
- It is not always easy to decide where in your organisation the ultimate responsibility for day-to-day Data Protection compliance should lie, but it is important to locate it somewhere.

Further information

Information Commissioner

The Information Commissioner produces guidance on the Act, and on a range of common specific issues. While not legally binding, this guidance is authoritative and – for the most part – succinct and well-explained. The most useful source of further information is therefore the Commissioner. For documents giving guidance on specific topics, see the 'Document library' on the website, accessible from 'Quick links'.

Wycliffe House, Water Lane, Wilmslow, Cheshire SK9 5AF
Web: www.ico.gov.uk
Switchboard: 01625 545700
Information line: 08456 306060/01625 545745
Notification
Tel: 01625 545740
E-mail: notification@ico.gsi.gov.uk.

Bates Wells & Braithwaite

Solicitors with a special interest in the voluntary sector, whose partners, Stephen Lloyd and Lawrence Simanowitz, have helped with this book.

2–6 Cannon Street, London EC4M 6YH
Web: www.bwbllp.com
Tel: 020 7551 7777

Criminal Records Bureau

Customer Services, PO Box 110, Liverpool L69 3EF
Web: www.crb.gov.uk
Information line: 0870 909 0811

Direct Marketing Association

The DMA operates the statutory telephone and fax preference services under contract, as well as the voluntary mailing preference service and other similar services.

DMA House, 70 Margaret Street, London WIW 8SS
Web: www.dma.org.uk
Tel: 020 7291 3300
E-mail: dma@dma.org.uk

Telephone and Fax Preference Services

DMA House, 70 Margaret Street, London WIW 8SS
Web: www.tpsonline.org.uk/www.fpsonline.org.uk
Subscriptions: 020 7291 3326 Complaints: 020 7291 3323
E-mail: tps@dma.org.uk/fps@dma.org.uk
To register a phone line not to receive unsolicited marketing: 0845 070 0707
To register a business fax line not to receive unsolicited marketing: 0845 070 0702
An online commercial number checking service is available at:
marketingfile.com/cleandata/default.asp

Institute of Fundraising

The Institute of Fundraising has a series of Codes of Practice on topics such as direct
mail and other aspects of fundraising which must comply with Data Protection, as well
as a Code on Data Protection itself.

Park Place, 12 Lawn Lane, London SW8 1UD
Web: www.institute-of-fundraising.org.uk/
Main switchboard: 020 7840 1000
Policy helpline: 0845 402 4771
Fax: 020 7840 1001

Institute of Fundraising Scotland

22/1A Calton Road, Edinburgh EH8 8DP
Tel: 0131 557 2100

Institute of Fundraising Cymru

1st Floor, 21 Cathedral Road, Cardiff CF11 9HA
Llawr Cyntaf, 21 Heol Y Gadeiriol, Caerdydd CF11 9HA
Tel/Ffon: 02920 340062 Fax/Ffax: 02920 521250

Legislation

For all current UK legislation see the Statute Law Database:
www.statutelaw.gov.uk

For European directives and other material, see:
ec.europa.eu/justice_home/fsj/privacy/index_en.htm

The UK government department with responsibility for Data Protection is the Ministry
of Justice:
www.justice.gov.uk

Training

Directory of Social Change
Holds regular training courses on Data Protection.
24 Stephenson Way, London NW1 2DP
Web: www.dsc.org.uk
Tel: 08450 777707
E-mail: training@dsc.org.uk

National Association for Voluntary and Community Action
Many local councils for voluntary service (CVS) organise training on how to comply with the Data Protection Act and/or can give advice. If you do not already know your local CVS, contact NAVCA:

The Tower, 2 Furnival Square, Sheffield S1 4QL
Web: www.navca.org.uk
Tel: 0114 278 6636
The website has links directly to the sites of local CVS.

Publications

The Russell-Cooke Voluntary Sector Legal Handbook, Sandy Adirondack and James Sinclair Taylor, Directory of Social Change, 2009: a comprehensive and authoritative guide to the law for voluntary organisations.

The Fundraiser's Guide to the Law, Bates, Wells & Braithwaite and Centre for Voluntary Sector Development, Directory of Social Change, 2000: all aspects of the law relating to fundraising.

Employment Records Handbook for Voluntary Organisations, Paul Ticher with Gill Taylor, Directory of Social Change, 2005: a detailed discussion of the record-keeping aspects of good employment practice and Data Protection compliance in respect of staff records.

Other books on Data Protection include:

Blackstone's Guide to the Data Protection Act, Peter Carey, Blackstone, 1998

Data Protection: law and practice, Rosemary Jay and Angus Hamilton, Sweet & Maxwell, 2007

Data Protection Act 1998: a practical guide, Heather Rowe, Tolley, 1999

Appendix A

Incorporation and charitable status

There is frequently confusion among those who work in voluntary organisations which are also charities about the relationship between incorporation and charity status. The following notes may be helpful.

Any organisation is either 'incorporated' or 'unincorporated'. There are several forms of incorporation; the commonest for voluntary organisations is a limited liability company. New forms, such as the community interest company (CIC), have recently become available and the charitable incorporated organisation (CIO) is, at the time of writing, shortly to become another option.

A commercial company is likely to be 'limited by shares': the members of the company are shareholders. Each owns a part of the company and usually receives dividends if it makes a profit. Trading companies linked to voluntary organisations are likely to be limited by shares. Normally the shares (or single share) are all held by the parent voluntary organisation or by trustees on its behalf.

For voluntary organisations themselves it is almost always inappropriate to be limited by shares. They will most likely be 'limited by guarantee'. The members in this case do not own the company, but they sign up to guarantee a small fixed amount (often £1) if the organisation cannot pay its debts when it is wound up.

All companies, whether limited by shares or guarantee, register with Companies House.

Limited liability, whether by share or by guarantee, means that if the company gets into debt, the individual members are highly unlikely to be held personally liable for the debt. In the vast majority of cases, all they will lose is the value of their shares or the amount of their guarantee. The members of the governing body (the company directors) are also protected from personal liability in most situations, but not all.

Another form of incorporation for voluntary organisations is an industrial and provident society.

All companies and industrial and provident societies are incorporated (which literally means 'made into a body'). Incorporation means that the organisation has its own legal existence and is a 'legal person'. It can enter into contracts, borrow money and be

178

sued, as though it were a human being (or 'natural person'). For Data Protection purposes this means that a company or industrial and provident society can have all the duties and responsibilities of a Data Controller in its own right.

An unincorporated organisation doesn't exist as a legal person. This means that technically it cannot properly meet the definition of a Data Controller. The Information Commissioner has indicated that for day-to-day purposes he will normally accept notification from an unincorporated association in its own name, and deal with it in other respects as a Data Controller. However, if it should ever come to legal action, this would most likely have to be taken against the trustees or management committee members individually.

If you are in any doubt about your organisation's status, you need to refer to the governing document. For a limited company this will be its 'memorandum and articles of association' (but for companies formed after 1 October 2009 it will be a single document called the articles of association). For an unincorporated association it will probably be a 'constitution' or 'rules'. For a trust (a form of unincorporated organisation) it will generally be a 'trust deed' or 'declaration of trust'.

Charity status

Charity status is a completely separate issue. A charity may be incorporated or it may be unincorporated. The issue in either case is whether its purposes are wholly charitable. If they are, it is a charity, with all the consequent obligations under charity law, including the requirement to register with the Charity Commission in most cases if it is based in England or Wales, the Office of the Scottish Charity Regulator (OSCR) if it is based in or operates in Scotland, and (from April 2010) the Charity Commission for Northern Ireland (CCNI) if it is based in Northern Ireland.

If an organisation's purposes are not wholly charitable, it cannot be a charity, even should it wish to be.

The easiest way to find out if your organisation is a registered charity is to see if it is listed in the Register of Charities on the websites of the Charity Commission (www.charitycommission.gov.uk), OSCR (www.oscr.org.uk) or CCNI when it is established. If you are still in doubt about whether the organisation is charitable – or if you think it should be registered but is not – contact the Charity Commission, OSCR or CCNI for further advice. Charities which are not registered with the Charity Commission, OSCR or CCNI generally need to be registered with the charities unit of HM Revenue & Customs. The Charity Commission, OSCR or CCNI can advise about this.

Charitable status has no effect at all on your Data Protection responsibilities, although various special provisions for non-profit organisations are described in the text of this book. All charities are non-profit organisations, but so are voluntary organisations which are not entitled to charitable status.

Appendix A

The new legal structures

A CIC can be a company limited by shares or by guarantee. The main differences from an ordinary company are that its memorandum and articles of association require it to act in the interests of the community, and if it is wound up its assets must be given to another CIC or to a charity. The obligation to act for the benefit of the community and the 'asset lock' make it similar to a charity, and a CIC can even have objects which are wholly charitable. But even with charitable objects, a CIC is by definition not legally charitable.

A CIO combines charitable status with the advantages of incorporation, without having to register with both Companies House and the Charity Commission/OSCR/CCNI. A CIO registers only with the charity registration body.

For Data Protection purposes CICs and CIOs are the same as any other incorporated body.

Appendix B

Schedule 3 Conditions for processing sensitive personal data

1 The data subject has given his explicit consent to the processing of the personal data.

2 (1) The processing is necessary for the purposes of exercising or performing any right or obligation which is conferred or imposed by law on the data controller in connection with employment.

   (2) The Secretary of State may by order –

   (a) exclude the application of sub-paragraph (1) in such cases as may be specified, or

   (b) provide that, in such cases as may be specified, the condition in sub-paragraph (1) is not to be regarded as satisfied unless such further conditions as may be specified in the order are also satisfied.

3 The processing is necessary –

   (a) in order to protect the vital interests of the data subject or another person, in a case where –

   (i) consent cannot be given by or on behalf of the data subject, or

   (ii) the data controller cannot reasonably be expected to obtain the consent of the data subject, or

   (b) in order to protect the vital interests of another person, in a case where consent by or on behalf of the data subject has been unreasonably withheld.

4 The processing –

   (a) is carried out in the course of its legitimate activities by any body or association which –

      (i)   is not established or conducted for profit, and

      (ii) exists for political, philosophical, religious or trade union purposes,

  (b) is carried out with appropriate safeguards for the rights and freedoms of data subjects,

  (c) relates only to individuals who either are members of the body or association or have regular contact with it in connection with its purposes, and

  (d) does not involve disclosure of the personal data to a third party without the consent of the data subject.

5   The information contained in the personal data has been made public as a result of steps deliberately taken by the data subject.

6   The processing –

  (a) is necessary for the purpose of, or in connection with, any legal proceedings (including prospective legal proceedings),

  (b) is necessary for the purpose of obtaining legal advice, or

  (c) is otherwise necessary for the purposes of establishing, exercising or defending legal rights.

7 (1) The processing is necessary –

    (a) for the administration of justice,

    (aa) for the exercise of any functions of either House of Parliament,

    (b) for the exercise of any functions conferred on any person by or under an enactment, or

    (c) for the exercise of any functions of the Crown, a Minister of the Crown or a government department.

  (2) The Secretary of State may by order –

    (a) exclude the application of sub-paragraph (1) in such cases as may be specified, or

    (b) provide that, in such cases as may be specified, the condition in sub-paragraph (1) is not to be regarded as satisfied unless such further conditions as may be specified in the order are also satisfied.

8 (1) The processing is necessary for medical purposes and is undertaken by –

    (a) a health professional, or

    (b) a person who in the circumstances owes a duty of confidentiality which is equivalent to that which would arise if that person were a health professional.

  (2) In this paragraph 'medical purposes' includes the purposes of preventative medicine, medical diagnosis, medical research, the provision of care and treatment and the management of healthcare services.

9 (1) The processing –

    (a) is of sensitive personal data consisting of information as to racial or ethnic origin,

(b) is necessary for the purpose of identifying or keeping under review the existence or absence of equality of opportunity or treatment between persons of different racial or ethnic origins, with a view to enabling such equality to be promoted or maintained, and

(c) is carried out with appropriate safeguards for the rights and freedoms of data subjects.

(2) The Secretary of State may by order specify circumstances in which processing falling within sub-paragraphs (1)(a) and (b) is, or is not, to be taken for the purposes of sub-paragraph (1)(c) to be carried out with appropriate safeguards for the rights and freedoms of data subjects.

10 The personal data are processed in circumstances specified in an order made by the Secretary of State for the purposes of this paragraph.

Additional conditions laid down by regulation

Under Condition 10 above, The Secretary of State has issued Statutory Instrument 2000 No. 417, the Data Protection (Processing of Sensitive Personal Data) Order 2000. This contains a range of provisions, of which (4), (7) and (9) may be particularly relevant to voluntary organisations.

Circumstances in which sensitive personal data may be processed

1 (1) The processing –
  (a) is in the substantial public interest,
  (b) is necessary for the purposes of the prevention or detection of any unlawful act, and
  (c) must necessarily be carried out without the explicit consent of the data subject being sought so as not to prejudice those purposes.
 (2) In this paragraph, 'act' includes a failure to act.

2 The processing –
  (a) is in the substantial public interest,
  (b) is necessary for the discharge of any function which is designed for protecting members of the public against –
    (i) dishonesty, malpractice or other seriously improper conduct by, or the unfitness or incompetence of, any person, or
    (ii) mismanagement in the administration of, or failures in services provided by, any body or association, and
  (c) must necessarily be carried out without the explicit consent of the data subject being sought so as not to prejudice the discharge of that function.

3 (1) The disclosure of personal data –
  (a) is in the substantial public interest,
  (b) is in connection with –

> (i) the commission by any person of any unlawful act (whether alleged or established),
>
> (ii) dishonesty, malpractice or other seriously improper conduct by, or the unfitness or incompetence of, any person (whether alleged or established), or
>
> (iii) mismanagement in the administration of, or failures in services provided by, any body or association (whether alleged or established),

(c) is for the special purposes as defined in section 3 of the Act, and

(d) is made with a view to the publication of those data by any person and the data controller reasonably believes that such publication would be in the public interest.

(2) In this paragraph, 'act' includes a failure to act.

4   The processing –

(a) is in the substantial public interest,

(b) is necessary for the discharge of any function which is designed for the provision of confidential counselling, advice, support or any other service, and

(c) is carried out without the explicit consent of the data subject because the processing –

> (i) is necessary in a case where consent cannot be given by the data subject,
>
> (ii) is necessary in a case where the data controller cannot reasonably be expected to obtain the explicit consent of the data subject, or
>
> (iii) must necessarily be carried out without the explicit consent of the data subject being sought so as not to prejudice the provision of that counselling, advice, support or other service.

5   (1) The processing –

(a) is necessary for the purpose of –

> (i) carrying on insurance business, or
>
> (ii) making determinations in connection with eligibility for, and benefits payable under, an occupational pension scheme as defined in section 1 of the Pension Schemes Act 1993,

(b) is of sensitive personal data consisting of information falling within section 2(e) of the Act relating to a data subject who is the parent, grandparent, great grandparent or sibling of –

> (i) in the case of paragraph (a)(i), the insured person, or
>
> (ii) in the case of paragraph (a)(ii), the member of the scheme,

(c) is necessary in a case where the data controller cannot reasonably be expected to obtain the explicit consent of that data subject and the data controller is not aware of the data subject withholding his consent, and

(d) does not support measures or decisions with respect to that data subject.

(2) In this paragraph –

    (a) 'insurance business' means insurance business, as defined in section 95 of the Insurance Companies Act 1982 F3, falling within Classes I, III or IV of Schedule 1 (classes of long-term business) or Classes 1 or 2 of Schedule 2 (classes of general business) to that Act, and

    (b) 'insured' and 'member' includes an individual who is seeking to become an insured person or member of the scheme respectively.

6 The processing –

    (a) is of sensitive personal data in relation to any particular data subject that are subject to processing which was already under way immediately before the coming into force of this Order,

    (b) is necessary for the purpose of –

        (i) carrying on insurance business, as defined in section 95 of the Insurance Companies Act 1982, falling within Classes I, III or IV of Schedule 1 to that Act, or

        (ii) establishing or administering an occupational pension scheme as defined in section 1 of the Pension Schemes Act 1993, and

    (c) either –

        (i) is necessary in a case where the data controller cannot reasonably be expected to obtain the explicit consent of the data subject and that data subject has not informed the data controller that he does not so consent, or

        (ii) must necessarily be carried out even without the explicit consent of the data subject so as not to prejudice those purposes.

7 (1) Subject to the provisions of sub-paragraph (2), the processing –

    (a) is of sensitive personal data consisting of information falling within section 2(c) or (e) of the Act,

    (b) is necessary for the purpose of identifying or keeping under review the existence or absence of equality of opportunity or treatment between persons

        (i) holding different beliefs as described in section 2(c) of the Act, or

        (ii) of different states of physical or mental health or different physical or mental conditions as described in section 2(e) of the Act, with a view to enabling such equality to be promoted or maintained,

    (c) does not support measures or decisions with respect to any particular data subject otherwise than with the explicit consent of that data subject, and

    (d) does not cause, nor is likely to cause, substantial damage or substantial distress to the data subject or any other person.

  (2) Where any individual has given notice in writing to any data controller who is processing personal data under the provisions of sub-paragraph

(1) requiring that data controller to cease processing personal data in respect of which that individual is the data subject at the end of such period as is reasonable in the circumstances, that data controller must have ceased processing those personal data at the end of that period.

8 (1) Subject to the provisions of sub-paragraph (2), the processing –
   (a) is of sensitive personal data consisting of information falling within section 2(b) of the Act,
   (b) is carried out by any person or organisation included in the register maintained pursuant to section 1 of the Registration of Political Parties Act 1998 F4 in the course of his or its legitimate political activities, and
   (c) does not cause, nor is likely to cause, substantial damage or substantial distress to the data subject or any other person.
 (2) Where any individual has given notice in writing to any data controller who is processing personal data under the provisions of sub-paragraph (1) requiring that data controller to cease processing personal data in respect of which that individual is the data subject at the end of such period as is reasonable in the circumstances, that data controller must have ceased processing those personal data at the end of that period.

9 The processing –
   (a) is in the substantial public interest,
   (b) is necessary for research purposes (which expression shall have the same meaning as in section 33 of the Act),
   (c) does not support measures or decisions with respect to any particular data subject otherwise than with the explicit consent of that data subject, and
   (d) does not cause, nor is likely to cause, substantial damage or substantial distress to the data subject or any other person.

10 The processing is necessary for the exercise of any functions conferred on a constable by any rule of law.

Appendix C

References, police checks and the Criminal Records Bureau

References

There is no legal obligation to provide an employment reference. If you do decide to provide one, you owe a duty of care both to the subject of the reference and to the prospective employer. In other words, the reference must not be too good, encouraging the employment of an unsuitable candidate, nor too bad, denying someone the chance to get a job they are suitable for, nor may it give a misleading impression.[69]

To ensure you comply with Data Protection requirements, you may want to have a policy on the type of reference you are prepared to provide. This could range from not giving references at all, through a mere statement of the fact that the person worked for you between certain dates in a certain capacity, up to a full reference with comments on their quality of work and so on. Having made your policy, you should then ensure that the records you keep when someone leaves are 'adequate, relevant and not excessive' for this purpose (and any other reason for retaining them). They must also, of course, be accurate. This could mean disposing of a lot of raw material and consolidating it on to a single summary sheet.

The Data Subject does not have the right to see a *confidential* reference by means of a Subject Access request to the provider of the reference. They may, however, make an application to the recipient. This Data Controller then, of course, has to apply the 'third

---

69 For more on references see *The Russell-Cooke Voluntary Sector Legal Handbook* or the *Employment Records Handbook*.

party' rule (see Chapter 13). If the provider of the reference is an individual who is identifiable to the Data Subject, and refuses consent, and is being reasonable, then access may be withheld.

To avoid complications, it is good practice to specify when requesting a reference whether you expect it to be provided in confidence, and kept confidential, or to be accessible to the Data Subject.

The Criminal Records Bureau

Under the 1984 Data Protection Act some employers adopted the practice of checking job candidates' criminal records by requiring them to apply for Subject Access to their own records and provide a copy to the prospective employer. This was not illegal, but it was not regarded as good practice, since the Subject Access request could reveal information such as 'spent' convictions, which the Data Subject would normally not be required to disclose.

The 1998 Act makes it illegal to force anyone to make a Subject Access request once an alternative means of checking someone's criminal record is available through the Criminal Records Bureau (CRB).[70] After much delay this eventually became partially operational in 2002 – and immediately became swamped with a backlog. As a result, the system of criminal records checks is still, at the time of writing, not in full operation.

The CRB provides for three levels of certificate:

- a **basic disclosure,** also known as a Criminal Conviction Certificate. This type can be obtained only by the individual, and shows only 'unspent' convictions. Implementation of this level of disclosure has been postponed indefinitely;
- a **standard disclosure,** or Criminal Record Certificate. These show cautions and 'spent' convictions as well as 'unspent'. They apply to occupations such as working with children or vulnerable adults, teaching, medicine and accountancy;
- an **enhanced disclosure,** or Enhanced Criminal Record Certificate. This includes additional material, including acquittals and police intelligence, and is available for a small number of jobs such as regular unsupervised work with children.

Disclosures contain 'sensitive' data, and misuse of the information or allowing anyone to have access to the information without a legitimate reason could clearly cause harm to the Data Subject. Use of disclosure information must be fair and secure, and the CRB Code of Practice says that data must not normally be retained after the decision has been made. The main Data Protection implication is therefore that there may be a need to record that an appropriate disclosure was obtained, but it is unlikely that any

---

70 In Scotland, the same functions are carried out by Disclosure Scotland.

information about an employee's actual criminal record would need to be kept unless other legislation (the Care Standards Act, for instance) requires the data to be held.

Generally, one organisation is not allowed to accept a disclosure previously issued to an individual for a post in a different organisation. Disclosing the contents of a CRB check to another organisation is not permitted in the CRB Code, which means that an organisation wishing to make use of a previous CRB disclosure – in the limited circumstances where this is possible – should obtain it only from the Data Subject directly.

Appendix D

Using photographs

The use of photographs and video material raises numerous issues. Although many of these are not directly linked with Data Protection, the questions are often raised in the context of Data Protection and related policies. This Appendix gives a short summary which may be helpful. Each of the following points should be taken into account when deciding to use photographs, especially of clients, but also of staff or volunteers, or members of the public attending events.

The following discussion refers to photographs. Similar considerations apply to video material (but not CCTV; this is a separate issue on which the Information Commissioner has issued a specific Code of Practice).

This is by no means a full statement of the law. You are strongly recommended to take specialist professional advice on the issues raised here.

Copyright[71]

Copyright normally belongs either to the person who takes the photograph or to their employer (if the photograph is taken during the course of their employment). Copyright can be 'assigned', and to make the assignment legally effective there is usually a payment, though this may be a nominal sum (even £1 is sufficient). This means that the person who holds the copyright transfers their rights completely to someone else. This should be done in writing.

If you want to reproduce material for which you do not hold the copyright, you must get a licence (permission) from the copyright holder. This may or may not require payment, and it may be for a single specific use, for a whole class of uses (e.g. non-commercial) or even for all possible uses. There may be conditions to the licence, often including acknowledgement of the copyright every time the material is reproduced.[72]

---

71 There is more on copyright in *The Russell-Cooke Voluntary Sector Legal Handbook.*
72 For example, the web version of the 1998 Data Protection Act states: '© Crown Copyright 1998. The legislation on this website is subject to Crown Copyright protection. It may be reproduced free of charge provided that it is reproduced accurately and that the source and copyright status of the material is made evident to users. It should be noted that the right to reproduce the text of Acts of Parliament does not extend to the Royal Arms and the Queen's Printer imprints.'

Copyright exists whether or not it has been claimed through the use of the © symbol. Where possible, it is sensible to indicate who owns the copyright on the back of a photograph or in the caption, and the year the photograph was taken.

Where the photograph is taken

There is generally no restriction in the UK on taking photographs in public places. However, people have a right to privacy; in private places they can legitimately object to photographs being taken. It is not always easy to tell whether a place is public or private. The more restriction there is on entry, the more likely it is to be private.

Clearly an advice session, a training course that participants had to sign up for in advance, or a staff party would be private, but a bring-and-buy sale which anyone could walk into on payment of 50p might not be.

The best thing, of course, is to make sure that people know you are going to be taking photographs and give them the option of not appearing in them. That way, you don't have to worry about whether your picnic in the park is a public or private setting. You can inform people in any appropriate way: a notice in the programme for the event, a notice at the door, a public announcement after everyone has taken their places, or making sure that the photographer asks for people's permission before taking their picture.

You should, of course, make sure that people know not just that photographs are being taken, but also what they will be used for, and how to avoid appearing in them.

What you use a photograph for is important. Even if taking a photograph is allowed, that does not mean you can automatically use it in any way you like. For example, you can defame someone by printing a picture of them in a situation that implies something negative and untrue about them – illustrating a story about benefit fraud, for example, with photographs of innocent people, even if you don't claim explicitly that the people are cheats.

Are the people 'identifiable'?

If any people in your photograph are so far away and their faces, clothes and 'shape' are so indistinct that they are not identifiable, there is almost certainly no restriction on what you can use it for. Equally, there are no Data Protection considerations.

However, if anybody is one of the subjects of the photograph, and if they are closer than full length, they are quite likely to be identifiable. There may still be no Data Protection implications, if the photograph is not 'data', i.e. is not on computer or in a structured set (see Chapter 3). Most photography nowadays is digital, however, so that even a single photograph might well be data. There is also, of course, the question of whether *you* can identify them. If you can't (and have no likely prospect of ever being able to find out who they are), then the data might not be 'personal'; again Data Protection would not apply.

But what if you publish a photograph not knowing who is in it? Consider the situation where photographs of your street party appear in your community association newsletter. Someone local sends a copy to a friend who has moved away. That person sees in one of the photographs their ex-partner arm in arm with someone else and this prompts them to take violent revenge. It doesn't take much imagination to see that there are circumstances when people would prefer their pictures not to appear in print, but you have no way of knowing this; assumptions can be dangerous.

You also need to be careful about using photographs without permission in case the person in the photograph has since died. It would no longer be Personal Data, perhaps, but the relatives might still be upset.

Artistic, literary and journalistic purposes

There is a specific exemption from fair processing, and most of the other Data Protection Principles, for 'artistic, literary and journalistic' purposes. However, the exemption only applies if:

- the material is eventually going to be published; and
- the Data Controller believes that the processing is in the public interest on grounds of freedom of expression; and
- compliance with Data Protection is incompatible with the photographs' purpose.

These conditions mean that the exemption is unlikely to apply to any use of photographs in the majority of voluntary sector publications. There will very rarely indeed be any overriding reason to ignore Data Protection.

Commercial use

If you want to use a photograph for commercial purposes, it would be sensible to square it with anyone who is identifiable in the photograph. Normally consent is obtained through a 'model release form' where the subject(s) of the photograph agree that it can be put to commercial use, usually for a fee.[73] Clearly an advertisement for a product would be commercial use, and a person whose photograph was taken in the street might be able to claim compensation for damage or distress caused by subsequent use of it in an advertisement without their knowledge or consent. But what about a brochure advertising your services, or promoting your organisation? You may decide that it would be best to get a model release form to be on the safe side.

---

73 An alternative approach is taken by some commercial attractions, for example, where the booking conditions specifically require you to waive any rights you may have over commercial use of photographs taken of people visiting the attraction.

Consent

Even for non-commercial uses, it is often good practice to get consent from the subjects of photographs. If you are putting photographs on a website, the risks are greater (see Chapter 18).

When you decide that consent is necessary, you should take the following factors into account.

- Be clear about what you intend to use the photographs for.
- Be clear about how long you will expect the consent to last. People who are happy to be associated with your organisation now may not be so keen in a few years' time when their interests or situation have changed.
- Make sure that you get accurate information to identify the people correctly.
- Make sure that you know how to contact people in case you may want additional consent for further uses in future.
- Make sure that anyone who gives consent on behalf of someone else is authorised to do so.

Designing databases that take Data Protection into account

When you ask an employee, volunteer or contractor to design or modify a database, you should ensure that they do as much as possible to help you comply with the Data Protection Act by building in specific features. The following is not necessarily an exhaustive list of points to cover, but may provide a good starting point.

- You must be able to retrieve and print out absolutely all the information about a particular individual easily and in a comprehensible form, in case they make a Subject Access request.
- You must build in appropriate security measures, including access controls and back-up procedures.
- Where you hold sensitive data you should think about placing this on a screen which can only be accessed by those who need to see it or, at least, which is not visible when the record is first called up and during routine processing such as mailings.
- You must be able to keep track of people who have opted out of direct marketing, and then suppress their record when you run mailings.
- You may also need to record opt-outs from disclosure to other organisations and opt-ins to telephone marketing, e-mail marketing and fax marketing.
- You should think about recording whether and how consent was given by the Data Subject for the use of their data, particularly sensitive data.
- If the database is used for more than one purpose, you probably need to record which purpose(s) were specified to the Data Subject at the time the information was collected.

- You should think about making provision to record the source of the information and any disclosure of it. This is not always relevant, but could be, especially if it is not obvious.
- You should think about how you monitor when records were created and updated, to help you comply with the requirements that information be up to date and not held longer than necessary.
- You may need to think about procedures for automatically removing or flagging information you are no longer sure about, or no longer need.
- Any database linked to the web in any way, or designed to exchange data with other organisations, needs to take account of the restrictions on transferring information abroad.
- You may need to record whether you have told people that you are processing information about them, and why. (If not, you may need to insert the relevant statement into your next communication with them.)
- You should think about how you brief users – either on-screen, in training materials or in printed documentation – about what the data is for, how it can legitimately be used and who is allowed to do what with it.

Index